# GoPro®
# Cameras

FOR

DUMMIES®

A Wiley Brand

# GoPro® Cameras

### FOR
## DUMMIES®
#### A Wiley Brand

by John Carucci

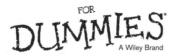

# Contents at a Glance

# Table of Contents

*Part III: Movies Are Made in Postproduction............... 143*

# Introduction

$C$ ompared with traditional camcorders, the GoPro is a superhero, able to leap tall buildings in a single . . . err, remote-control action. Your first inclination when hearing about such a unique camera is that it has to cost a lot of money, but that's not the case. The GoPro is cheap. Very cheap.

The GoPro challenges conventional notions of where you can put a camcorder and continually encourages users to find new and exciting places to capture movies. It's waterproof, so you can capture video footage under the wettest of circumstances, submerging the camera to record stunning underwater sequences. Even the lowest-priced model comes with a waterproof housing.

The capability to work in weird places would go only so far if the GoPro's image quality were subpar. In fact, the GoPro captures high-definition (HD) video at a rate of at least 30 frames per second (fps), depending on the model, so you can capture unique high-quality video at an affordable price.

Some GoPro models are also capable of capturing 4K video — the successor to HD, with double the quality.

This rugged little camera can go anyplace and produce exciting new perspectives. It works for everyone from amateurs to pros. Families use it to document their daily lives; students experiment with it; photographers use it to supplement camcorder footage. GoPro has even spread to the professional arena, with an increasing presence in broadcast news programs, movies, and television shows.

I've had a blast making movies and playing with my GoPro, so I hope you'll think that I'm the right dummy to introduce you to this camera.

## About This Book

*GoPro Cameras For Dummies* helps you make sense of GoPro moviemaking. Through my experience as a still photographer and a television producer, I describe how to use your GoPro to make movies, take still images, and make time-lapse sequences.

Think of this book as a quick information stop where you can find out what you need and get back to work. It includes cinematic tips, effects that will impress your audience, advice on effective edits, and even some cool uses for your GoPro.

I wrote this book for people who have different proficiency levels. Some readers have already made their mark in conventional video production and want to add one more weapon to their arsenal. Others come from the still-photography sector and are fascinated by the GoPro's still and time-lapse capabilities. Hobbyists, family documentarians, and students are all looking to understand this new, exciting phenomenon. The goal of this book is to make sure that everyone gets the knowledge he or she needs to use the GoPro.

# How This Book is Organized

*GoPro Cameras For Dummies* is divided into four parts; each part details the phases of understanding GoPro moviemaking as effectively as possible. You will no doubt have a preference for a particular area. You may relish the section that pertains to the understanding the camera to make a movie, or you may skip ahead to the filmmaking techniques or the cool places you can use a GoPro.

## Part I: Getting Started with Your GoPro Camera

This section provides you with a swift overview of the capabilities of the GoPro camera system. Whether you're a beginner looking to make movies with this unique camera, a working professional looking to create fresh visual perspectives for your movie or segment, or anyone in between, this group of chapters covers the device and important accessories needed for making movies.

## Part II: Moviemaking Technique

Regardless of the device or camera, the language of cinema remains the most important aspect for making a movie. The chapters in this part explain fundamental filmmaking techniques to you so that you can produce an impressive movie with your GoPro.

## Part III: Movies Are Made in Postproduction

After understanding your GoPro and using time-honored techniques to shoot your movie, it's time to put it all together. This part covers editing your movie with GoPro Edit software or other programs, such as Adobe Premiere or Apple Final Cut Pro.

## Part IV: The Part of Tens

The *For Dummies* version of a top ten list provides insight into some common and unusual places to use a GoPro and professional uses.

## Icons Used in This Book

What's a *For Dummies* book without icons pointing out great information that's sure to help you along your way? In this section, I briefly describe the icons used in this book.

This icon marks a generally interesting and useful fact — something you may want to remember for later use.

This icon points out helpful suggestions and useful nuggets of information.

When you see this icon, you know that techie stuff is nearby. If you're not feeling very techie, feel free to skip it.

The Warning icon highlights lurking danger. With this icon, I'm telling you to pay attention and proceed with caution.

## Beyond the Book

Understanding your GoPro goes beyond these pages and onto the Internet, where you can access additional information. There's a handy-dandy cheat sheet that reiterates the basics and web extras.

- **Cheat Sheet:** You can find this book's online Cheat Sheet at `www.dummies.com/cheatsheet/goprocameras`. See the Cheat Sheet for tips on getting started with your GoPro, shooting your masterpiece, and using GoPro Studio Edit.

- **Web Extras:** Companion articles to this book's content are available at `www.dummies.com/extras/goprocameras`. The topics range from mastering the GoPro mindset, creating stylish movies, and ten ways to capture great GoPro video.

- **Updates:** If this book has any updates, they'll be posted at `www.dummies.com/extras/goprocameras`.

# Part I
# Getting Started with Your GoPro Camera

getting started
with

GoPro cameras

## In this part . . .

- ✔ Understand the GoPro camera.
- ✔ See what you need to get started.
- ✔ Find the right mount.
- ✔ Set up your GoPro.

# Getting to Know GoPro

## In This Chapter

▶ Discovering GoPro

▶ Finding out what GoPro can do

▶ Comparing models

▶ Working with the GoPro App

You've probably heard the old saying, "Good things come in small packages." Sometimes it's true, as in the case of a diamond ring. That sparkly rock is definitely small, and many people would agree that it's good. But a mosquito, which is smaller than a diamond, isn't good at all, especially on a warm summer evening.

Small cameras rarely solicit as much disdain as mosquitoes do. Most of us accept the compromise of function for size, understanding that it's acceptable for a camera to have less quality and fewer features in exchange for traveling well.

The GoPro, however, shatters that compromise like a rock on a plate-glass window. This pint-size wonder not only fits in the palm of your hand, but also easily mounts anywhere. Put it on a bicycle helmet to capture the rider's perspective. Mount it on a surfboard and not worry about frying the electronics, thanks to its watertight housing. How about mounting it on an inexpensive remote-control drone (more appropriately known here as a quadcopter) and recording overhead footage — something that was out of the realm of possibility for consumers a few short years ago? (Check local ordinances first so you don't fly your airship too close to a restricted area or violate privacy and security of others. More on that in Chapter 3.)

## Introducing the GoPro

The GoPro is a pint-size, consumer-priced camcorder that yields professional results and does lots of cool stuff thanks to its Wi-Fi capability, superior performance, and extreme portability.

The GoPro doesn't take up much space, so it's easy to pack, carry, and mount in interesting places. It's a shade under 3 inches long (with the waterproof housing), so it would take a bagful of these cameras to occupy the same amount of space as a conventional camcorder. Its diminutive stature becomes even more important when you mount several GoPro cameras in a confined area — and that's a good thing, because these little guys are often used in bunches.

"The bigger they are, the harder they fall" doesn't apply to the GoPro because it weighs ounces, not pounds. Because the camera is small and lightweight, you can place it almost anywhere with little concern that it will fall because it's too heavy.

Earlier GoPro models captured movie files on an SD card, but because the camera gets smaller and lighter with each upgrade, it now uses a very petite microSD card (see Figure 1-1).

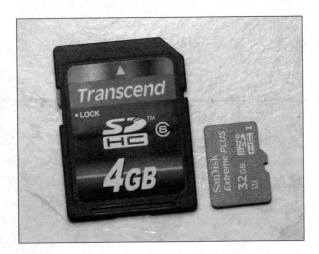

Figure 1-1: SD (left) and microSD (right) cards.

Wishing for the existence of such a camera just a mere generation ago was quite a stretch, like wanting a Pegasus in your barn. Fret no more. Your sanity is safe — at least when it comes to the existence of a durable, inexpensive camera that goes anywhere while capturing high definition video and even 3D video. All it takes to accurately capture whatever situation you have in mind is an optional, inexpensive mount.

## Use it anywhere

Just a few years ago, ambitious users who attempted to put an expensive camcorder in a place where it didn't belong usually didn't get a compelling piece of work; rather, they often had to pick up the pieces of their smashed cameras. That's less a worry these days, thanks to the design and durability of the GoPro.

Beyond being small and well designed, a GoPro can go anyplace you go and mount almost anywhere. Moviemaking has always had the dubious distinction of being a cumbersome endeavor, usually because of the size and weight of the equipment. It's quite refreshing to have a high-quality camera with ultra-wide optics that fits in the palm of your hand and that has a mount for almost every situation.

Going in nonconventional places is the GoPro's job description. The tougher the location, the better. The GoPro is shock-resistant and waterproof, which are pretty good qualities for a camera that can mount on almost anything, moving or otherwise. The next time you're inspired to mount the camera on Fido for a dog's-eye view, feel free. Shock your friends and neighbors when you decide to take the camera into the pool to shoot an underwater sequence. You don't even have to worry about a waterproof housing, because it comes standard with the camera (see Figure 1-2).

## Forget conventional camcorders

The GoPro doesn't resemble a conventional camcorder, as you can see in Figure 1-3; neither does it behave like one. It looks more like a small square box with a protruding lens than a sleekly designed camcorder. Although you can hold it like a traditional camera, it's more comfortable to hold when it's attached to something.

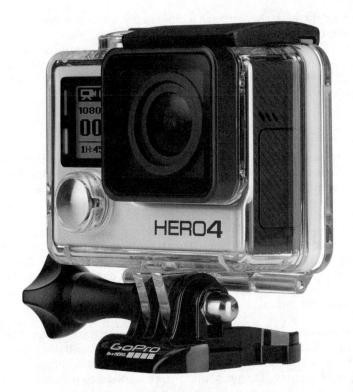

Figure 1-2: GoPro Hero4 in waterproof housing.

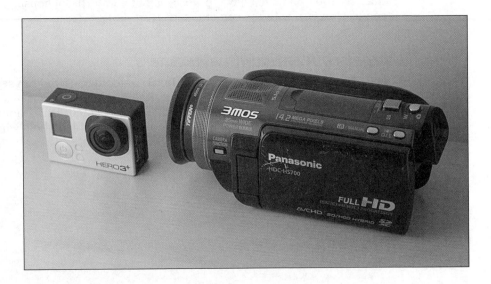

Figure 1-3: GoPro and Panasonic HD camcorder side by side.

TIP

Here are some of the qualities that differentiate a GoPro from standard camcorders:

- **Size:** The current GoPros are quite small compared with most camcorders and significantly smaller than their predecessors.

- **Most models don't have a viewfinder:** Though the viewfinder is one of the main parts of a camcorder, only one current GoPro includes a viewing screen. That's okay because you wouldn't look through a viewfinder for most situations. The lack of a viewfinder doesn't mean you have to imagine where the action will take place. Simply use the GoPro App (discussed later in this chapter), which transforms your smartphone or tablet into a monitor.

- **Wide-angle view:** You won't find a zoom lens. Instead, the GoPro uses a fixed 170-degree lens that provides an ultra-wide view unavailable on any camcorder.

TECHNICAL STUFF

Just a few years ago, merely having a moderate wide-angle view on a camcorder was a minor coup. Going reasonably wider often meant using one of those poor quality wide-angle adapters that screwed on the filter or clamped over the lens. Adapters produced exaggerated distortion, especially on the edges, creating a foggy appearance. The GoPro provides a wider perspective than those old accessory lenses, as shown in Figure 1-4, and does it with impressive optical quality.

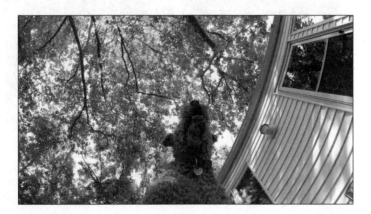

Figure 1-4: Pretty view from the GoPro's fixed-focal-length wide-angle lens.

- **Waterproof housing:** Take your camcorder out in the rain, and pray that doesn't die. Attach it to a surfboard, and read it its last rites. Not so with the GoPro. Thanks to its clear polycarbonate housing (with glass lens), you can use a GoPro in, around, and under water. The waterproof case is rated shockproof and waterproof up to 131 feet. The Dive Housing can go even deeper.

✔ **Wearability:** Though it's not the kind of accessory that fashionistas clamor for on the catwalk during Milan Fashion Week, the GoPro is still quite fashionable. You can not only wear it, but also capture some pretty impressive video with it. Here are a few ways to wear it:

• *Headband:* The headband attaches to your head so you can get that walk-through look in your video.

• *Wristband:* The wristband looks like a wristwatch, as you can see in Figure 1-5. Capture timely footage simply by twisting your arm.

• *Bicycle helmet:* Wear the camera on your head to get the unique perspective of a cyclist.

• *Body harness:* The harness allows you to transform yourself into a living dolly. Instead of moving the camera through the scene and capturing choppy footage, be one with the camera and move through the scene in Zenlike splendor.

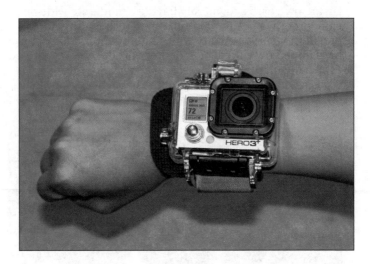

Figure 1-5: GoPro on a wristband.

In a way, the GoPro represents the elusive go-anywhere camera that's everything the camcorder never was: durable, mountable, and affordable.

## Seeing What a GoPro Can Do

What can a GoPro do? Here's a more relevant question: What do you want it to do? Asking this question is more like asking yourself about your own wishes and desires for unique video footage. When you determine what you want to capture, all you have to do is connect the camera to the appropriate mount and press the Record button.

The following sections cover a few special capabilities of the GoPro.

## Take still photos

Although still-photo capability rarely (and *rarely* means almost never) finds its way onto the list of reasons to buy a video camcorder, GoPro is the refreshing exception to that rule. It not only gets up close and personal with its ultra-wide-angle view (see Figure 1-6), but also does it with extreme sharpness. You can take still capture even further by capturing a scene at preset intervals to create a time-lapse movie. Although the current editions of the GoPro have excellent still photo quality, it increases with each model.

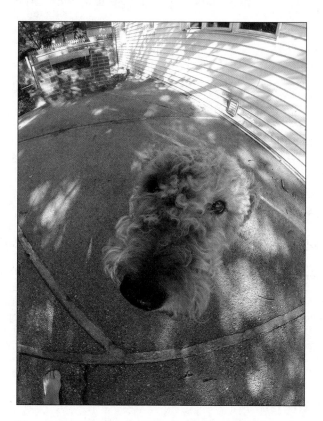

Figure 1-6: Still capture with the GoPro is remarkably good.

For details on still-photo specs, see "Comparing the Hero4 and Hero3+ Editions" later in this chapter.

## Capture the scenes of your dreams

The GoPro liberates your imagination by allowing you to capture situations that in the recent past seemed like fantasies. Since the early days of motion-picture capture, people always had the desire to present each shot with a unique perspective. At some point or another, we've all wanted to mount a video camera on a car bumper to capture compelling footage or fly it remotely over the action on some hobby craft, but doing so was never feasible or practical. The ambitious efforts of the more adventurous often ended in a crash landing.

Now, with GoPro, those creative ideas are not only possible, but also practical thanks to the camera's durability, unique mounts, and Wi-Fi communication. Here are a few things that GoPro makes possible:

- Connect it to an extension pole to get an overhead shot of the scene.
- Put it on a guitar.
- Mount it on a car.

## Capture HD and 4K video

Although all current GoPro models let you capture full-frame high-definition (HD) video, the quality and frame-rate options increase with the Silver and Black editions (see "Comparing the Hero4 and Hero3+ Editions" later in this chapter). Using H264 compression, the GoPro compresses captured video files to fit more information on the microSD media card, and the compressed files maintain substantial quality when opened.

4K is a high-resolution setting for video capture. Think HD and then double the quality. Only the Black Edition has the capability to capture 4K video, making it one of the most affordable cameras of this type on the market.

The 4K mode captures 3820x2160 resolution with a frame rate of 30 frames per second (fps) on the Hero4 Black Edition. The higher frame rate cuts down the choppiness when capturing action sequences. The Hero4 Silver Edition and Hero3+ Black Edition capture at 15 fps. The HD modes on all current Hero models capture between 30 and 120 fps. The more frames a camera captures, the smoother the playback. At 15 fps, situations that have less movement render much better than those with fast action.

## Attach to anything

The GoPro system can make you feel like Inspector Gadget. There's something very spylike about securing your GoPro anyplace you want — high or low, moving or stationary — and then monitoring the scene on your smartphone. Thanks to the camera's various mounting plates, you can put it almost anywhere.

Connect the camera to a skateboard, or mount a bunch of cameras inside and outside a car as it plows through dunes (see Figure 1-7). You can even hold a GoPro underwater with an extension pole to capture underwater video. I talk more about mounting devices in Chapter 3.

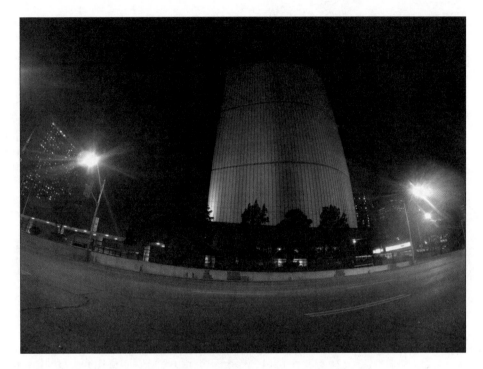

Figure 1-7: GoPro on a roll-bar mount attached to a pole captures this night scene.

## Connect to your other devices

Wi-Fi capability doesn't mean you can check your fantasy-football scores when shooting, but it does provide some pretty radical communication between the camera and your smartphone or remote. You can control the camera over Wi-Fi with your smartphone, view footage on your tablet, and use either device as a monitor. About the only thing you can't use it with is a real-time monitor because of the delay.

Here's what you can do via Wi-Fi:

- Update firmware.
- Check battery level.
- See microSD card info.
- View still photos and video.

# Comparing the Hero4 and Hero3+ Editions

The latest GoPro line — Hero4 — features three cameras with varying features and quality levels. Each model offers Wi-Fi capability.

## Hero4 Black Edition

The big kahuna of the Hero line offers the latest and greatest technology in a GoPro. With advancements in video capture, image processing, and new features, it allows you to do more cool things than ever before. Here are some of its new and improved features:

- **Beyond HD capture:** Captures 4K video at 30 fps as well as 2.7K at 50 fps for ultra high-resolution capture.

- **HD video capture:** Captures HD video at up to 1080p (progressive) at 120 fps, making it possible to capture maximum detail even when applying slow-motion in GoPro Studio.

- **More powerful processor:** Twice as fast as its predecessor, so you can capture video at increased frame rates with more detailed image quality, increased sharpness, and better color.

- **Auto Low Light:** Automatically adjusts exposure by changing frame rates to compensate when you move between dense shadow areas and bright spots.

- **Protune for photos:** Apply the same control over images as you have for video. Change the ISO setting, use exposure compensation, or adjust white balance on still images and time-lapse sequences.

- **Built-in Wi-Fi and Bluetooth:** Allows you to control the camera remotely, using the Wi-Fi remote with the GoPro App. For this model, the remote is sold separately.

- **Set tags on your video:** The HiLight tag makes it easy to find the best part of your clip by setting markers while capturing footage.

The Hero4 and Hero3 Black Editions also come in two specialized configurations:

- **Surf:** This bundle provides everything you need to attach your GoPro to a surfboard, providing video content that wasn't possible a decade ago. The camera comes bundled with a surfboard mount and tethers that securely anchor the camera with extra layers of protection. It includes the remote control.

- **Music:** If capturing a unique perspective for a live musical performance is your thing, this bundle can work for you. It includes a clamp, removable instrument mounts, and a 3.5mm miniplug cable. This bundle doesn't include the remote control.

## Hero4 Silver Edition

The most versatile member of the Hero line is the first GoPro to have a view-finder, along with its share of new, improved features. The Silver Hero4 also comes in Surf and Music configurations. Some of its new and improved features include:

- **Beyond HD capture:** Captures 4K video at 15 fps.

- **HD video capture:** Captures HD video at up to 1080p (progressive) at 60 fps, making it possible to capture maximum detail even when applying slow-motion in GoPro Studio.

- **Auto Low Light:** Automatically adjusts exposure by changing frame rates to compensate when you move between dense shadow areas and bright spots.

- **Protune for photos:** Apply the same control over images as you have for video. Change the ISO setting, use exposure compensation, or adjust white balance on your still images and time-lapse sequences.

- **Built-in Wi-Fi and Bluetooth:** Allows you to control the camera remotely, using the Wi-Fi remote with the GoPro App. For this model, the remote is sold separately.

- **Set tags on your video:** The HiLight tag makes it easy to find the best part of your clip by setting markers while capturing footage.

## Hero3+ White Edition

The most vanilla camera (and lowest-priced) of the GoPro Hero3 line still provides formidable results, offering HD video capture, still-photo mode, and a waterproof housing. It's a modified version of the Hero2, but a little bit smaller, with built-in Wi-Fi.

Here are some of its other features:

- **HD video capture:** It captures HD video at up to 1080p (progressive) at 30 fps. It also captures 960p video at 30 fps and 720p video at 60 fps.

- **Ultra-wide-angle lens:** It provides a 170-degree angle of view.

- **Still-image capture:** It provides 5MP (megapixel) capture with a burst of 3 fps. Time-lapse mode lets you capture a series of photos at intervals of .05 to 60 seconds.

- **Built-in Wi-Fi:** This feature allows you to control the camera remotely, using the Wi-Fi remote with the GoPro App. For this model, the remote is sold separately.

- **Portability:** It's hard to beat a camera that comes with a protective housing that's wearable, mountable, and waterproof to 131 feet.

## What the numbers mean (and the letter too)

The different settings for your GoPro refer to the resolution, more specifically, the horizontal resolution. The more lines the better the quality. HD has a resolution of 1920x1080 lines, vertical and horizontal, respectively. Resolution settings use the horizontal setting. The "p" refers to the resolution being *progressive.* That means it shows the entire image at once, as opposed to interlaced, or with an "i" at the end. The "i" stands for *interlaced,* meaning the picture consists of flickering lines. Just think back to looking at the screen of an old tube television and you'll know what I mean. The progressive signal offers better image quality.

If you're on a budget, and still-image capture isn't a top priority, you can't go wrong with the White Edition. It can also keep your budget grounded when you're buying additional GoPro cameras for specific shoots.

### Hero3+ Silver Edition

More than just a step up from the White Edition, the Silver Edition is a lighter version of the Black Edition. (The Gray Edition? Well, no, but you get the idea.) Tonal assignment aside, this model provides better performance, increased frame rate for video capture, better still-image capture, and faster Wi-Fi than the White Edition.

Here are some advantages of the Silver Edition:

- **Better video capture:** Offers more options for picture quality, including a high-frame-rate capture at 1080p60, 960p60, and 720p120 video modes. This results in professional-quality footage and allows for liquid-smooth slow-motion playback. The Silver Edition has an upgraded sensor that delivers improved low-light performance.

- **Powerful photo capture:** Excellent for still photography because it can capture a 10MP image at up to 10 frames per second. That makes it perfect for fast-action sequences.

- **Enhanced low-light performance:** The upgrade sensor performs well in dimly lit situations.

- **Sharper lens:** Improved optics help produce increased image sharpness and fewer artifacts.

- **Improved audio:** Features upgraded audio performance that captures sound more accurately. It also includes advanced wind-noise reduction for clearer audio during high-speed activities.

- **Longer battery life:** The Silver Edition has the longest-lasting battery of the current Hero3+ line due to lower resolution.

> ✔ **Faster Wi-Fi:** The Silver has much faster Wi-Fi than the White Edition does. How much faster? Try four times. Previewing your shot from a distant location and sharing video are much faster when you use the GoPro App. The optional Wi-Fi remote lets you control up to 50 cameras from up to 600 feet away.

If you're looking for slightly better video quality and technology than the Hero3 White Edition offers, and if you're willing to spend about $100 more, this model is a fair compromise.

## Hero3+ Black Edition

Standout features of this model include

✔ **Improved video quality:** Offers more options for picture quality including higher resolution choices and frame rate capture at 1440p at 48 fps, along with 1080p60, 960p100, and 720p120 video modes for capturing the best-quality footage.

✔ **Beyond HD video capture:** The Black Edition lets you capture 4K video at 15 fps as well as 2.7K at 30 fps for ultra high-resolution capture.

It's not easy to notice the quality difference between HD and 4K unless you're viewing the video on a 4K television set. The experience isn't much different from shooting a movie in HD and watching it on an analog television set. Still, it's nice to know that you can shoot 4K when you want it.

The Black Edition also includes a 2.7K setting, which is between HD and 4K and uses the more refined 30 fps setting. Once again, you can't really appreciate viewing it on an HD television.

✔ **Impressive photo capture** Lets you capture impressive 12MP stills, and can shoot fast action sequences in succession up to 30 frames per second. The Time Lapse mode lets you capture motion at intervals between 0.5 and 60 seconds. Continuous Photo shoots full-resolution stills at a steady 3, 5, or 10 frames per second when holding down the shutter button.

✔ **SuperView (Black Editions, Hero4 Silver Edition):** Get more headroom out of the lens by capturing a 4x3 aspect ratio and dynamically stretching it to a 16x9 aspect ratio. This allows you to capture more of the scene.

✔ **Auto Low Light mode:** Automatically adjusts for low-light situations by changing frame rates to alter exposure. In a way, it's like altering exposure levels on a conventional camera by raising or lowering the shutter speed to let more or less light into the lens.

✔ **Includes Wi-Fi remote:** Besides the 4K capability and otherwise better performance across the board, the Black Edition includes the optional remote. It lets you completely control up to 50 GoPro cameras that are closer than 600 feet away. It's compatible with the other models, but you need to purchase it separately.

TIP

If you have the budget and want 4K capability, increased photo-capture quality, or grandiose features like 3D capture (using two cameras and a special mount), the Black Edition is truly a no-brainer. It does more than any other GoPro and also includes the otherwise-optional remote control. If you feel it's necessary to have the remote control, you're better off buying the Black Edition because the cost of the remote control is close to the difference in price between the Black and Silver Edition.

## Using the GoPro App

The GoPro App (see Figure 1-8) allows you to control the camera from a distance and monitor the scene. It also lets you wirelessly update camera firmware and get the latest features to maintain best performance. The app lets you control the camera and do more with your content than ever before, including sharing it over social media. It provides full remote control of all camera functions so you can start and stop your recording, adjust camera settings, or take a photo.

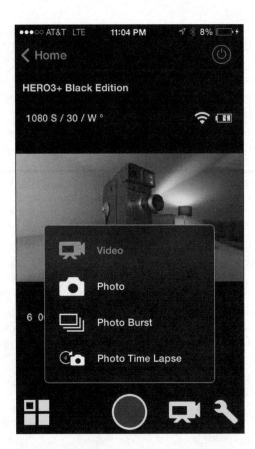

Figure 1-8: GoPro App.

Live Preview (see Figure 1-9) lets you see what your camera sees for easy shot framing while capturing the scene. You can also play back video and view photos right on your smartphone.

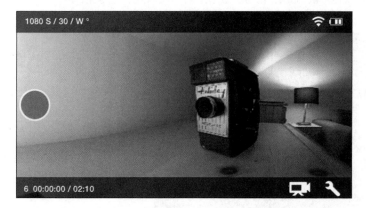

1080 S / 30 / W °

6  00:00:00 / 02:10

**Figure 1-9:** Live monitoring of a scene with the GoPro App.

Updating firmware on electronics isn't for the faint-hearted. It's complicated and bothersome, and nobody really wants to do it, so it doesn't always get done. The GoPro App, however, changes all that by allowing you to keep your camera up to date via Wi-Fi.

You can share your favorite video clips and photos via email, text, Instagram, Facebook, and other social networking sites. Although you can't share directly from the camera, you can use the app on your smartphone or other mobile device to access the image files and then share them (see Figure 1-10). It's a free download at `http://gopro.com`.

---

# Challenges in using a GoPro

GoPro does so many things well — such as capturing HD video at a high frame rate and shooting high-quality time-lapse sequences — that it's easy to forget that using it involves some challenges:

✔ Steep learning curve

✔ Lower quality in low light

✔ Short battery life

✔ Fixed focal length

✔ Few controls on camera

✔ Lack of a viewfinder on most models, making it harder to compose the scene

✔ A lag of 2 to 3 seconds when you monitor a scene on a mobile device

✔ Not easy to hold in your hands like a conventional camera

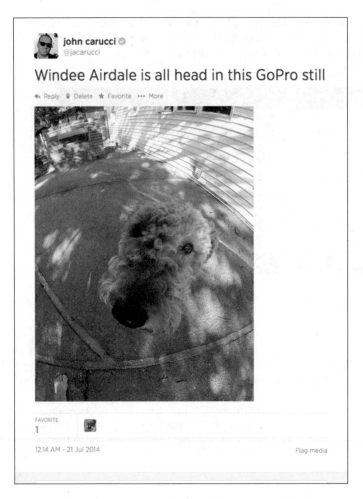

**Figure 1-10:** Shared image on Twitter transferred from GoPro App.

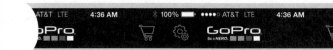

# Shooting Out of the Box

## In This Chapter

▶ Unpacking your camera

▶ Seeing how everything works

▶ Acquiring the GoPro App

▶ Working with the remote

▶ Mounting your camera

*W*hile it's bold to say that GoPro offers the most revolutionary way for consumers to make movies, it's also a bit of an understatement. The camera offers a wide-angle view that has not been affordable for still photographers, and non-existent for videographers. When you add its waterproof housing, a relatively low price (from a couple of hundred bucks), and a wide array of mounts to place it just about anywhere, it changes the way we make movies.

There are so many things you can do with this diminutive marvel, but unlike conventional camcorders or cameras, it's important to get familiar with your GoPro from the time you remove it from the package to when you download your movies and still photographs. This chapter examines the GoPro's features and operation.

## Setting Up Your GoPro

At first glance, the GoPro resembles a miniature version of an early 20th-century box camera or maybe the Instamatic still camera of the 1970s. Its design is simple: nothing more than a small box with a protruding lens, a few buttons, and a small LCD screen up front on most models. One model, the Hero4 Silver Edition, offers a built-in screen. This chapter shows you how everything works.

## Taking it out of the box

There's an art to taking electronic devices out of their packages; some items require near-surgical pursuit to remove.

Although it's not terribly hard to remove your GoPro from its package, take care not to rip it out. You could do some serious damage. Please be gentle.

Although it may seem ridiculous to describe how to take a camera out of the box, the following easy instructions show you how to expedite the process without doing any damage:

1. **Remove the small adhesive disk that holds the box sleeve to the plastic casing.**

2. **Slide the sleeve off.**

3. **Separate the top plastic case from the box.**

   Pull the tab and peel away the tape that connects the plastic case to the box, as shown in Figure 2-1.

4. **Do one of the following:**

   • If you have the Hero3+ Black Edition, open the box top (with the words *GoPro* on it); open the ties to release the remote and then close the box again.

   • If you have any other edition, skip to Step 5.

   After you take the plastic cover off the top and expose the camera, it's still attached to the top of the box that it sits on. Don't pull it off. Think of this as your first lesson in the GoPro mounting system.

5. **Squeeze the mount below the camera, and slide the camera off.**

   This step leaves the mount attached to the box. Keep the box, because it can serve as an extra mounting plate if you ever need one. You can glue it or screw it to just about anything to make your own mounting solution.

6. **Take all the pieces out of the box (such as the battery, mounts, and rings) and lay them out, as shown in Figure 2-2.**

One very important piece *doesn't* come with the camera: the microSD card. Guess what? The camera won't work without it. Ideally, you purchased one when you bought your GoPro. If not, get one before you set up your camera (see the next section).

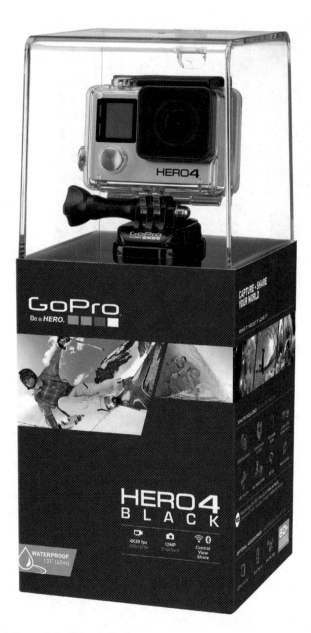

**Figure 2-1:** GoPro in the box.

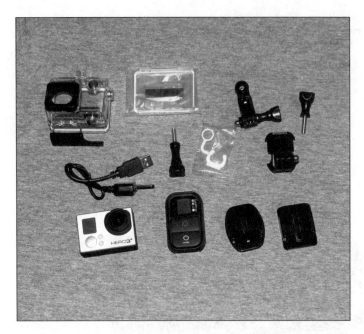

Figure 2-2: The camera and all its pieces.

## Getting it up and running

Setting up your GoPro takes a few minutes (not counting battery-charging time) but is pretty easy. Follow these steps:

1. **Take off the GoPro's protective waterproof housing.**

   Like a turtle uses it shell for protection, so does the GoPro. But you need to take the GoPro out of its case to set it up. Pull the black latch on the top front of the camera. You'll need to pull it back hard because it locks in place. Lift the latch and pull out the camera.

2. **Put the battery in the camera.**

   Slide off the battery door, place the battery inside the camera, and put the door back on. The battery comes partially charged and can be used right out of the box, but it's a good idea to charge it fully (see Step 4).

3. **Load the microSD memory card.**

   The door on the side of the camera slides off. Push the tiny card into the card slot until it locks in place. Then slide the door back on.

## There's always a GoPro charger

Because the camera uses a USB mini connector, those old cell phone chargers used by BlackBerry and others work perfectly with charging the camera. So take them out of the drawer when you need an AC charger for your camera.

**4. Charge the camera.**

Plug one end of the charger cable (the one with the mini USB plug) into the camera and the other end into your computer or USB power supply. While the camera is charging, the LED lights turn on; when the camera is fully charged, they go off.

**5. Charge the remote by using the other charger cable.**

That is, if the model you purchased comes with a remote. For detailed directions, see "Using the GoPro Remote" later in this chapter.

**6. Power up the camera.**

Press the Power/Mode button. The LED indicators blink, and the camera beeps three times.

**7. Shoot some video.**

Once your camera is charged, you're ready to start recording. The video mode is the default mode when you turn on the camera. Press the Shutter/Select button to record video; press it again to pause it.

**8. Take a still photo.**

Press the Power/Mode button to find the Photo button, which looks like a camera. You can also pick other still photo choices like Burst Photo and Time Lapse, but more on that in Chapter 4.

## Controlling Your GoPro

If you're a first-time user, you'll find that the GoPro differs from any other camera you've operated. The lack of a viewfinder (except for the Hero4 Silver Edition), the camera's fixed ultra-wide-angle lens, and its dependence on Wi-Fi take a bit of adjustment.

The GoPro has only three buttons:

✔ **Power/Mode:** This button acts as both a power button and a means of cycling through camera modes and menus.

✔ **Shutter/Select:** Press this button to start and stop video recordings, take photos, and toggle among menu settings.

✔ **Wi-Fi:** To turn the camera's Wi-Fi signal on or off, hold this button for three seconds. This button also allows you to enter the Settings menu, connect to the remote, or connect to smartphones and tablets via the GoPro App.

## Knowing what the lights do

The camera has five LED indicator lights. Those red and blue lights make the GoPro look pretty cool, but they also serve specific purposes:

✔ The bottom-front LED blinks red to indicate video recording and photo capture.

✔ The top-front LED blinks blue to show that Wi-Fi is activated.

✔ The LED lights on the top, bottom, and side of the camera blink red to indicate recording or Wi-Fi status.

## Turning the camera off

Powering down your GoPro requires you to hold the Power/Mode button for a few seconds. Whatever you captured will be saved before the camera powers off. Also keep in mind that if the memory card is full or the battery is out of power, the GoPro automatically stops recording and powers off. In that situation, your video will be saved before the camera powers off.

## Setting the date and time

Not setting the date and time on your camera would be the equivalent of not setting the clock on a DVR. All your pictures, including the ones you took during the summer, would be dated January 1.

Setting the date and time is simple. Just power up the camera and follow these steps:

1. **Press the Power/Mode button until you get to the Settings menu — the one that looks like a wrench.**

2. **Press the Shutter/Select button to enter the Settings menu.**

3. **Cycle through the Settings menu by pressing the Power/Mode button until you get to get to the Setup menu; then press the Shutter/Select button.**

4. **Scroll through the Setup menu until you get to calendar mode; then press the Shutter/Select button.**

   Calendar mode is easy to find because the icon looks like a calendar.

5. **Press the Shutter/Select button to select Month, press the Power/Mode button to scroll to the correct month, and press the Shutter/Select button to select it.**

6. **Repeat Step 5 to set the day, year, hour, and minute.**

### Syncing your GoPro

Your GoPro connects to your smartphone or device via Wi-Fi so that you can control the camera, clear the media card, and update its firmware when necessary. More important, the GoPro App provides a comfortable way to use the camera because chances are you're not always going to be that close to the action, and if you are, then you can concentrate on what you're doing. You can read more about the GoPro App later in the chapter.

## Working with the GoPro App

The GoPro App is the heart and soul of the GoPro operation. Here are some of the things it lets you do:

- Operate the camera from 50 feet away.
- Monitor the scene on your smartphone's screen.

    Don't expect monitoring to be perfect. There's a bit of lag time between the camera and your smartphone — as much as a few seconds. To judge the delay, put your hand in front of the camera's lens and then take it away, and see how long it takes for the change to appear on your smartphone.

- Control one camera or multiple cameras, with all the technical settings at your disposal.
- Select the mode you want to capture.
- Start and stop video recording, take still photos, and do time-lapse photography.
- Erase a full memory card or delete just the last item captured.

One caveat: The app doesn't work when the camera is underwater. You can still record — by tapping the app's Shutter/Select button before submerging the camera — but you won't be able to monitor the scene.

### Downloading the software

The GoPro App is a free download away. Just go to Apple's App Store, the Windows Store, or Google Play. You can find more information at http://gopro.com on the Software and App page.

## Setting up the app

Here's how you set up the app:

1. **Activate Wi-Fi on the camera by pressing the Wi-Fi button on the side.**

   The blue light blinks to show that Wi-Fi is activated.

2. **Open the GoPro App on your smartphone and then tap the Connect & Control button, shown in Figure 2-3.**

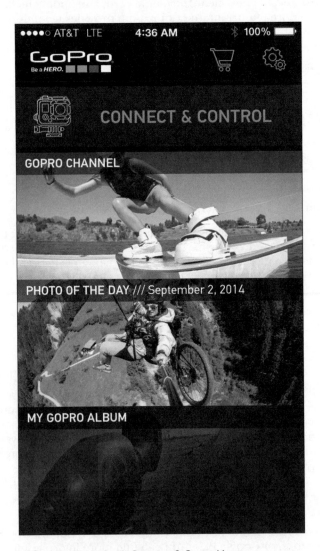

Figure 2-3: GoPro App's Connect & Control button.

3. **If you see a No Cameras Connected warning, navigate to the Wi-Fi settings on your smartphone and make sure that the GoPro is selected.**

   Often, your home Wi-Fi network is selected by default on your phone, and you need to select the camera.

4. **Control the camera.**

   Monitor the scene and make changes without ever touching the camera. You can change camera modes, adjust resolution settings, and access Protune settings on the Black Edition.

### Giving the app a test drive

Although using the GoPro App is pretty intuitive, giving it a test drive doesn't hurt. Follow these steps:

1. **Launch the GoPro App.**

2. **Tap the Command & Control button.**

3. **Tap the video icon.**

   By default, the video icon should be selected, but if it's not, tap the icon that looks like a movie camera.

4. **Point the camera at something, and check the scene on the monitor.**

5. **Make camera adjustments, if necessary.**

   Chapter 4 offers detailed explanations of how these features work.

6. **Tap the red button to start recording video.**

7. **Tap the red button again to stop recording.**

## Using the GoPro Remote

If you don't want to use the GoPro App (see the preceding section), you can use the GoPro remote control, which works up to 600 feet from the subject and lets you control the camera from that distance. It's also waterproof up to 10 feet, making it great for water sports such as surfing and waterskiing. Keep in mind that you cannot use the remote and GoPro App at the same time.

Charging the remote takes a few minutes to figure out, so instead of wasting time, follow these steps.

1. **Remove the metal attachment key.**

   Slide the tab on the back as you pull out the metal attachment key.

2. **Connect the hooked end of the charging cable to the remote (see Figure 2-4).**

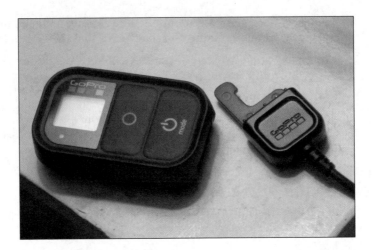

Figure 2-4: GoPro remote and cable.

3. **Plug the other end of the cable into a USB port on your computer.**

4. **When the LCD indicator on the remote shows that the remote is fully charged (via a battery icon), disconnect the charging cable, and reattach the metal ring.**

It's essential to put the ring back. If you don't, you won't be able to attach it to your key ring.

## Mounting Your GoPro

GoPro has a lot of mounts — one for every occasion and situation, as you see in Chapter 3. There are mounts for your ski pole, the roll bar of your all-terrain vehicle, and the top of your bicycle helmet. There's even one that your dog can wear as a harness.

I mention GoPro mounts throughout the book, but I take a little time here to explain the pieces inside the box that apply to mounting:

✓ **Pivot arms:** The pivot arms come in two varieties: straight and angled (see Figure 2-5). You use them to put the camera farther from the mount or to rotate it. When you add an angled extension, it changes the mount by 90 degrees, so each one that you add turns the camera. You can add as many arms as you need, joining them with the thumbscrews that come in the GoPro package.

✓ **Quick-release buckle:** You get two of them, one of which is slightly larger and more flexible than the other. The pivot arms attach to many of the mounts as well as the quick-release buckle that locks into some of the mounts. When using the quick-release buckle, you just slide and clip, as shown in Figure 2-6.

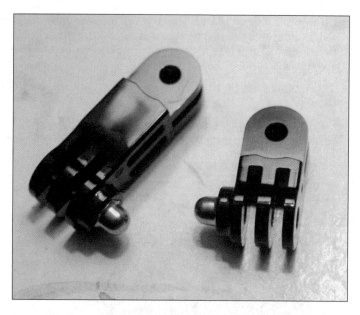

Figure 2-5: Pivot arms.

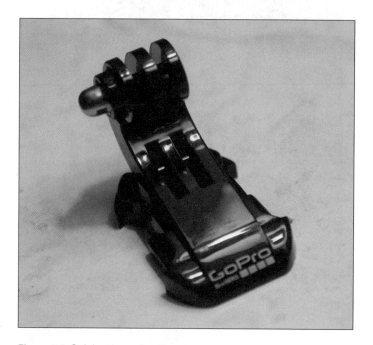

Figure 2-6: Quick-release buckle.

✔ **Double-stick base plates:** One of the adhesive mounts that accommodates the quick-release buckle is flat, and the other is slightly curved (see Figure 2-7). The quick-release buckle can be used with either adhesive mount.

These plates are permanent, so be sure to put them where you want them to stay.

Even though the base-plate seal is permanent, you may have to wait a while for it to set — as much as 24 hours during cold weather.

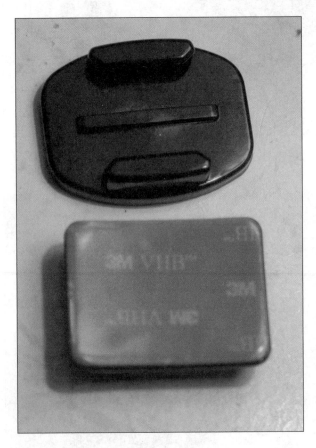

Figure 2-7: Base plates.

# 3

# Accessorize Me

Think about the potato for a second. The tuberous nightshade vegetable lacks the flavor that it has when it's cooked and spiced. Well-prepared potatoes are a much-loved food source that sometimes we love too much (thank you very much, French fries) and at other times just enough (boiled potatoes, you know who you are).

In a strange way, GoPro alone has much in common with a potato. Just as you can eat a raw starchy potato by itself, you can use a GoPro without any accessories. You can still take pictures and make movies with it. The problem is that you can't really mount the camera or monitor what you're doing with it.

GoPro seems like quite the accessory hound, but it includes a vital accessory right in the box: the waterproof housing. That's just the tip of the iceberg. Dozens of other accessories allow you to blaze new trails and do either the wildest or most practical things you can imagine.

## Playing the Media Card

It's important to make sure you can capture the action by using the right media card. Just as your grandmother used the very best grated cheese for her lasagna, you should use a microSD card that's optimized for video capture.

Not just any media card will do. Forget about capturing a continuous movie in high definition (HD) if you're not using the right type, and if you have your heart set on capturing 4K video, the plot thickens. Capacity plays a big part (as you see in this section), but speed matters most.

## Observing the speed limit

Because media cards have so many uses, the capacity of a card and the speed at which it transfers data will vary. Regardless of which kind of card you're using, here's a breakdown of the Speed Class Rating system, a system created by a consortium of manufacturers. You can find more information at www.sdcard.org.

- **Class 2:** 2MB per second
- **Class 4:** 4MB per second
- **Class 6:** 6MB per second
- **Class 8:** 8MB per second
- **Class 10:** 10MB per second
- **UHS Speed Class 1:** 10MB per second
- **UHS Speed Class 3:** 30MB per second

## Checking card capacity

HD movie files are large, and the 4K ones are even bigger. That's why it's important to have a large-capacity card so it doesn't fill up sooner rather than later. Today, microSD cards continue to increase in capacity while going down in price. But sometimes the difference in price between using the right card and a slower one isn't that much different. That's why you should purchase the card based on its speed and storage, and not because of its cost.

Not all Class 10 cards are created equal. They represent the minimum speed requirement, so even cards from the same manufacturer differ in speed.

Here are transfer speeds for a few popular cards that you can use with your GoPro:

- **Lexar 633x Class 10:** This card comes in three sizes — 16GB, 32GB, and 64GB — and offers a maximum transfer speed of 95MB per second.

- **Samsung Extreme:** This media card has capacity up to 64GB and transfer speed up to 70MB per second.

- **SanDisk Extreme:** SanDisk's Extreme Plus (see Figure 3-1) comes in three sizes: 16GB, 32GB, and 64GB. The Extreme Pro is faster, with speeds up to 95MB per second, but is available only in 8GB and 16GB versions.

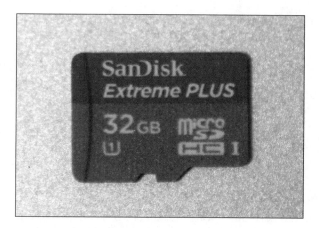

Figure 3-1: SanDisk 32GB Extreme Plus.

 GoPro can capture 4K video, which shows twice as much detail as HD. With great quality, however, comes great size. Capturing 4K video requires a fast, high-capacity card, because 4K takes up far more space than HD does. How much depends on the frame-rate setting. Regardless, 4K video is going to take up more than half of the capacity of the card, so a 32GB card with 4K video on it will hold less than a 16GB card would.

### Choosing the right card

The best type of card for you depends on what you're trying to do and on your budget. Still-image capture requires less transfer speed than video does, so if you don't have the fastest card, you can still get by. When you're shooting HD movies, though, you need a card with a write speed that can keep up with movie capture. Using a low-speed card is like having slow workers on a factory assembly line; it makes the operation less efficient.

 GoPro recommends SDHC cards with a minimum Class 10 rating. Slower cards will work, but they process moving images less efficiently. Also, there's always a risk that a slower card will lag and stop recording. Worse, you could lose data with a slow card. If you're doing 4K, consider UHS Speed Class 3 cards for seamless capture. They're the most expensive cards but are designed for the fastest transfer rates.

## Letting the GoPro Get Wet

One of the main reasons to buy a GoPro is to be able to take it into the sloppiest of conditions with little worry. You didn't have that choice with other camcorders. Taking a conventional camcorder through a swamp or shooting upward during a torrential rainstorm isn't in that device's best interest.

Chances are that you'd burn it out. Most conventional cameras — especially the electronic ones — don't like the wet stuff.

Being able to go underwater makes the GoPro is as refreshing as a cold glass of water or a swimming pool on a hot summer day — and you can adequately capture each of those locations from the inside out. Isn't it nice to have a camera that has the same tolerance for wet conditions as your diver's wrist-watch? Feel free to get it wet. Just don't take it in your bathtub without the waterproof housing, and make sure you don't have the Skeleton backdoor on. That one's not waterproof.

## Using underwater accessories

If you're looking to record underwater seascapes or artful pool pictures, GoPro lets you capture these submerged scenes with relative ease and little worry. Still, recording underwater is challenging. You won't be able to frame the shot if you can't see it. Normally, you could monitor the scene with your smartphone (see Chapter 2), but that's not feasible for underwater recording because of the whole water-is-wet thing. The optional Touch BacPac (see the next section) works pretty well, allowing you to monitor the scene from the back of the camera, but it's submersible only to shallow depths, and the touch panel won't work underwater.

Here are some accessories to consider for underwater recording:

- **Antifog inserts:** These inserts drop into the camera's housing to prevent fogging in cold and humid environments. You can reuse them several times by drying them out in a 300°F oven for 5 minutes.

- **A big media card:** You can't change the card underwater (or anywhere that's even slightly moist, for that matter), so it's a good idea to use the biggest one you can afford.

- **Color-correction filters:** Underwater scenes are beautiful, but they have blue or green casts. An optional color-correction filter in red or magenta can reduce or eliminate the cast.

- **Scuba mask:** The GoMask is a cool third-party accessory that lets you wear the camera on your face while snorkeling or scuba diving so you can see what you're capturing.

- **Video lights:** You can get a complete light system that mounts on a rack with your GoPro and provides up to 900 lumens of illumination for densely lit underwater scenes.

- **Floaty Backdoor:** This accessory attaches to the back of the camera and keeps it afloat. Any time you play in the water, there's a risk that the camera will take more of a plunge than you'd like. Thanks to this bright-orange back, however, you'll have no problem spotting it in the water.

✔ **Dive Housing:** The waterproof housing that comes with the camera works pretty well for most underwater situations, but if you want to take the camera deeper, consider this housing. It's more durable than the standard model and is waterproof to 197 feet. The kit includes Standard, Skeleton, and BacPac backdoors. Its increased durability makes it perfect for more serious diving encounters. And its glass lens delivers optimal sharpness in and out of the water.

✔ **Blackout Housing:** When you're shooting on land and want to remain inconspicuous, the Blackout Housing (see Figure 3-2) lets the camera blend into the scene unnoticed. Its matte black finish provides low visibility, allowing you to capture footage without drawing attention to the camera. LCD concealment stickers eliminate light reflection.

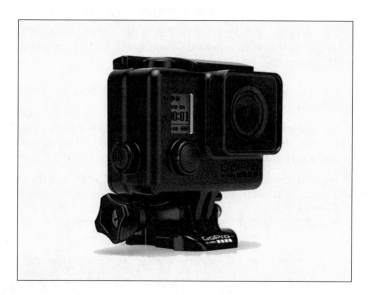

Figure 3-2: Blackout Housing.

## Going deep

Standard with every GoPro camera, the waterproof housing can withstand depths of up to 131 feet (40 meters). You can leave the housing on the camera when you're using it for non-water-based fun. (Actually, you need it for some mounting options, because they attach to the housing. But I'm talking about waterproof situations in this section.)

Two backdoors come with your GoPro: Skeleton, which provides good sound quality, and Standard, which is waterproof.

Make sure that you have the Standard backdoor on when you use the GoPro underwater, because the Skeleton isn't waterproof.

Here are the maximum depths your GoPro can reach with a couple of other accessories:

- **Dive Housing:** This accessory increases the GoPro's depth rating to 197 feet (60 meters).

- **Touch BacPac Backdoor:** There's a trade-off with this accessory. Although it lets you monitor the scene from the camera back, you can't use it deeper than 10 feet (3 meters).

## Checking your camera before getting it wet

Anytime you plan to take your GoPro in the water you need to be sure everything is correctly set *before* you submerge it. So before taking it for a dip consider the following:

- **Have enough room on the card:** Remember, if you run out of storage, you can't change cards in the water.

- **Make sure it's clean:** Not only do they say it's next to godliness, but keeping the glass in front of the lens clean will assure you capture clear and sharp images.

- **Test the case:** A test case *case?* Why not? Yeah. It's waterproof, but isn't nice to be reassured? So without the GoPro inside, close it up and submerge in water, as seen in Figure 3-3. After a brief soak, dry the outside completely before opening and see if it's wet inside.

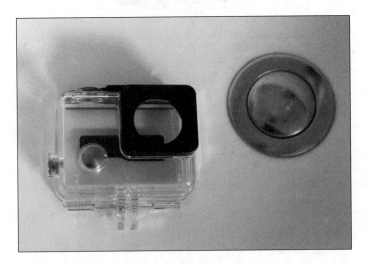

Figure 3-3: Testing the GoPro case in the sink, sans the camera.

- ✓ **Make sure the camera is fully sealed:** Push the housing backdoor all the way in before securing the black latch on the top of the case.

- ✓ **Rinse off salt water:** If you're going to take it to the beach, on a dive, or any situation involving salt water, it's always a good idea to safely remove the camera and wash the housing with fresh cool water. The salt can get caught in the case and around the lens, causing rust on the metal parts and a salty coating over the lens.

# Keeping the Shot Steady

The ability to place your GoPro almost anywhere makes it a pretty remarkable camera. But to capture all that action and those cool perspectives with little worry, you need to keep the camera steady. The GoPro isn't like any other camera; it's fairly tiny and, with the exception of one model (Hero4 Silver), doesn't have a viewfinder. Holding it in your hand to take a picture or make a movie is the textbook definition of haphazard, because you can't see what you're shooting or hold the camera comfortably.

You can mount a GoPro on a tripod or on any of the dozens of mounts designed for the GoPro. In this section, I give you an abridged tour of some exotic and basic mounts.

## Mounting your GoPro out of the box

When you take the camera out of the box, you'll notice that it comes with a bunch of small pieces of hardware:

- ✓ **Quick-release buckle:** Designed to connect the camera to the waterproof housing horizontally as well as attaching to a wide selection of mounts.

- ✓ **Arms:** Let you extend the camera and then tilt or twist its position.

- ✓ **Flat adhesive mount:** Makes it easy to connect your GoPro to any clean, flat surface. When the camera is attached to the quick-release buckle, it slides right into the mount.

- ✓ **Curved adhesive mount:** Looks a little like the flat mount but is designed for curved surfaces.

## Using a tripod (with an adapter)

For a good part of the camera's 200-year history, the tripod has been the photographer's best friend when it comes to keep the camera steady and composing the scene. For almost as long, cameras have had a standard socket for attaching to a tripod. Yep, the three-legged amigo has made all the difference between crisply shot movies and blurry messes.

One problem with the GoPro is that it doesn't have a tripod socket on its bottom, so there's no built-in way to secure the camera to a tripod. No worries. You can still mount it with a special accessory that attaches to your GoPro and provides a standard tripod socket. This accessory also has a quick-release mount that allows you to move the camera conveniently between shots and locations. The GoPro looks comfortable when mounted on a flexible GorillaPod, for example (see Figure 3-4).

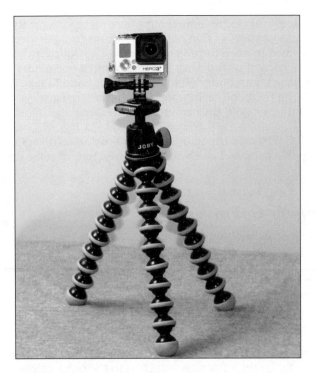

Figure 3-4: Tripod adapter connects a GoPro to a GorillaPod.

## Getting Framed

You can leave your GoPro in its waterproof housing for most situations, but sometimes you may want to shoot outside of the case. The Frame is a cool accessory that allows you to place the camera in a frame, as the name implies. The open design delivers optimal audio capture, providing it's not an activity that puts the camera too close to the noise. The integrated latch makes removing your GoPro from the Frame quick and easy. You also have open access to the camera's microSD, Micro HDMI, and USB ports for easy data offload, live-feed video, and charging.

Here are some reasons for using it:

- ✔ **Not bulky:** Because it fits around the camera, it doesn't add size to the camera like the waterproof housing.
- ✔ **Better audio capture:** Because the microphone is not obscured by the case, you get the clearest sound reproduction.
- ✔ **No waterproof housing:** Provides immediate access to camera ports for downloading data and live-feed video.
- ✔ **Protective glass lens:** Prevents the camera lens from getting dirty or scratched.
- ✔ **Extendable support arm:** Lets you easily attach accessories like the LCD Touch BacPac or Battery BacPac.

## Using suction cups

When you think of mounting your camera with suction cups, secure placement isn't the first thing that comes to mind. The first thing is "I hope it stays on," as you worry that the cup will lose suction and the camera will fall off.

Not gonna happen. The industrial-strength suction cup mounts attach the camera to almost any flat, clean surface — even the hood of a moving car, a motorcycle, or a boat. How reliable are they? These mounts have been engineered to withstand a broad range of motion at speeds in excess of 150 mph.

## Using the Jaws Flex Clamp

"Jaws Flex Clamp" sounds like a sequel to the shark thriller, but this accessory lets you attach your GoPro to anything it can bite . . . err, clip. The mighty little clamp lets you attach the camera to a variety of objects up to 2 inches thick. You can mount the camera directly on the clamp, or attach it to the optional gooseneck to accommodate a wider range of camera angles.

## Choosing your mounts

There's a mount specific to whatever you're looking to do with your GoPro, from surfing, skateboarding, playing music, or wearing it like a fashion accessory.

### 3-Way

You can use this mount, shown in Figure 3-5, in three ways: as an extension arm, camera grip (when detached from the arm), and tripod. This cool mount expands to 20 inches and collapses to 7.5 inches, and it's waterproof.

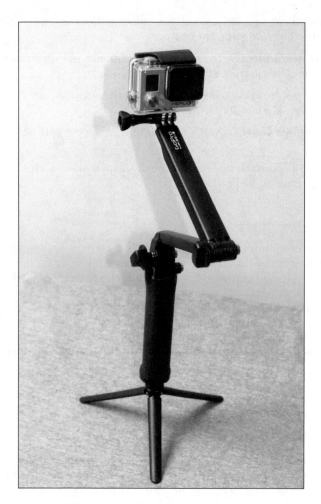

Figure 3-5: The GoPro 3-Way mount.

### Bar

No, it's not for capturing a movie at your favorite watering hole, though it's entirely possible to put one of these mounts around a beer tap or stool leg. This mount allows you to attach your GoPro to just about any kind of bar with a diameter of 0.75 to 1.4 inch. The included adapter lets you attach the camera to even narrower bars.

Put the camera on the handlebars on your bike or motorcycle, or a windsurfer or ski pole. The included pivot arm lets you adjust the camera to the perfect angle.

### Roll bar

The roll-bar mount is for much thicker bars, from 1.4 to 2.5 inches in diameter. That covers mountain-bike frames, go-karts, and even cars with roll bars.

### Sportsman

The Sportsman easily attaches the GoPro to sporting equipment such as a fishing rod, hunting rifle, or bow so you can capture all sorts of outdoor adventures.

The mount fits around anything with a diameter of 0.4 to 0.9 inch. The mounting point is on the back of the camera, not on the bottom.

### Musical mounts

Almost since the beginning of photography, musical performances have been captured from the outside, and the resulting footage often has a two-dimensional appearance. Musicians don't want a clunky camera intruding in their performance space. But the GoPro can go where other cameras can't, thanks to a few mounts specifically designed for music:

- **Microphone-stand mount:** This dandy little device transforms a microphone stand into a tripod of sorts. It's compatible with standard microphone stands when you use the included adapter. It comes with a quick-release base that allows you to move the camera between mounts and locations.

- **Instrument mount:** If you're looking to get a little closer to the action, opt for a removable instrument mount, which allows you to attach your GoPro to a guitar (see Figure 3-6), bass, drums, or keyboard. You can even mount it on a turntable, if spinning vinyl is your jam. These temporary mounts have nondamaging adhesive that's safe for most instrument surfaces. The kit includes three mounts (reusable) and two single-use adhesive strips.

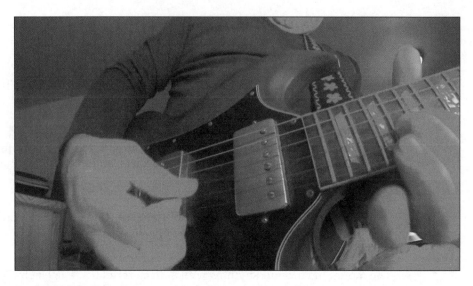

Figure 3-6: Guitar mount showing some up-close picking action.

## Wearing Your GoPro

First, the fashion was skinny jeans; then it was iridescent shoe soles; now it's wearing the GoPro like a fashion accessory. Perhaps the only fashionable aspect of wearing a GoPro is the ability to capture great video with an interesting perspective. Regardless of the trends of the day, great video is always in vogue.

GoPro offers a bunch of wearable mounting options that may not improve your attire but can certainly make your movies look better by showing a truly POV perspective (see Figure 3-7). *POV* stands for *point of view,* and it's yours that the viewer will see.

Why wear your GoPro? Because you can. More important, it's more feasible to mount the camera than to try to hold it. For one thing, your hands are a little too big for it. That makes taking pictures or shooting movies not much different from going to your 5-year-old niece's tea party with her dolls and drinking out of those tiny cups.

Another dilemma in holding the camera is that the angle of view is so wide, it's easy to get your hands, nose, or other parts of your body in the shot — and because most models lack a viewfinder, you won't know until it's too late. That problem is exacerbated when you try to use your smartphone to view and realize that you're a hand short. For those times when handholding is necessary, consider using the LCD Touch BacPac, which allows you to monitor the scene on the camera.

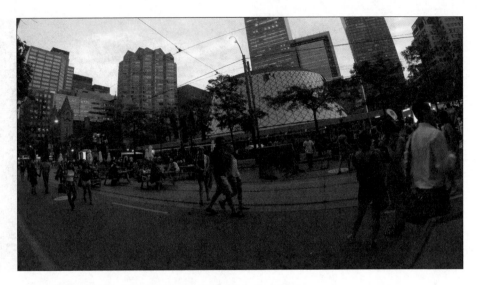

Figure 3-7: A POV shot taken while walking down the street.

The following sections cover a few accessories that can help you use your GoPro hands-free.

## Headband mount

If you want to capture video from the perspective of what you're seeing and want to look something like a coal miner too, this mount is for you. The fully adjustable strap allows you to attach the camera to your head or a helmet to capture footage from a headlamplike perspective. Thanks to its design, you can also put it on a baseball cap.

## Helmet mounts

Helmet mounts come in several configurations. If you're going to use this mount while riding a bicycle, always select a helmet that meets the applicable safety standard when you use with a GoPro helmet mount.

GoPro offers several helmet mounts, including these:

- **Helmet mount:** Whether you take your GoPro on a motorcycle ride down a country road or zip down a windy trail on your mountain bike, this mount allows you to record the view from atop your head, as shown in Figure 3-8. The camera sits on the helmet like a headlamp, letting you capture forward-facing footage. You can adjust the extendable arm so that the camera faces you for self-portrait videos and photos.

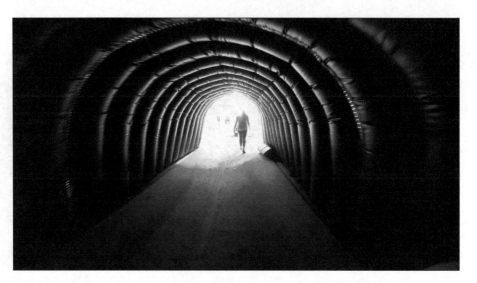

Figure 3-8: A helmet mount lets you capture forward-facing footage.

This mount uses a special adhesive that can be removed only by heat from a hair dryer.

- ✓ **Vented-helmet mount:** Instead of using adhesive to hold the camera in place, this mount uses straps to attach the camera to any vented sports helmet. The adjustable strap makes mounting the camera quick and easy.

- ✓ **Side mount:** You can do more than just attach your GoPro to the side of a helmet with this mount. It also works well on vehicles and other moving objects. Three-way adjustability makes aiming the camera easy.

- ✓ **Night-vision mount:** This mount allows you to attach your GoPro to a helmet that includes a mounting plate for Night Vision Goggles.

## Chest harnesses

Sometimes when you're in the middle of the action, it's nice to hold the GoPro near and dear to your heart — literally. The chest harness lets you wear the camera on your chest near your heart. Basically, it looks like suspenders with a camera in the middle.

This harness comes in two sizes:

- ✓ **Chesty:** This harness makes it easy to capture immersive video and photos. One benefit of using this type of mount is that you can include more of your body in the frame. It's perfect for immersing yourself in your favorite activities, such as mountain biking, motocross, skiing, or paddle sports. You'll capture more of your arms, knees, and maybe face (when you lean in). It's fully adjustable to fit a wide range of adult sizes.

✓ **Junior Chesty:** This smaller version of the Chesty is perfect for smaller humans, better known as kids. It lets them have fun with the GoPro when they're playing on slides and swings, or skateboarding or bicycling.

## Fetch (dog harness)

For too many years, our fine-feathered friends have gotten credit for the shot that looks down on the situation. Well, move over bird's-eye view and make way for the dog's life view. Think of the Fetch as the canine version of the Chesty, allowing you to record the world as seen from the back of your dog. You can use it on any dog between 15 and 120 pounds. Just make sure the dog is never left alone, and not just because she will claim credit for the footage.

## Wrist mount

The Wrist Housing lets you change the angle of view with a flick of the wrist. You wear this mount like a wristwatch, which makes it great for capturing footage on the fly, as shown in Figure 3-9. Simply move your wrist to change the angle. The housing secures the camera flat against your wrist and lets you pivot the camera upright to shoot photos or video. It fits over ski gloves and jackets.

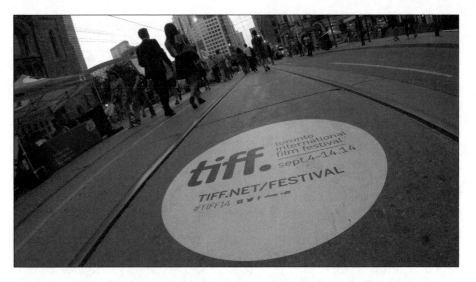

Figure 3-9: Wearing the camera on your wrist lets you swoop down on the subject.

# Keeping Your GoPro Charged

Your GoPro Hero camera offers amazing results while it's powered up, but unfortunately, the power doesn't last long. Battery life is less than two hours, which can pose a problem when you're out in the field. That's why it's a good idea to have an extra battery or two.

Here are a few other accessories that can keep your GoPro powered longer:

- **Battery BacPac:** For situations that require longer continuous service from the camera, you should consider using the Battery BacPac. This helpful accessory attaches to the back of the camera to extend battery life. Charge it through your computer or a wall charger. The LCD window displays battery level and charging status.

- **Dual-battery charger:** This device lets you charge two batteries at the same time and is USB-compatible. LED indicator lights display the charging status of both batteries.

- **Wall charger:** The wall charger lets you connect your camera via USB directly to an AC outlet for fast charging. You can record while charging, essentially plugging the camera into a continuous power source.

- **Auto charger:** This device allows you to charge up to two cameras in your car.

# Adding Some Other Cool Accessories

Not every accessory has to do with mounting your GoPro. Some of them enhance the camera's operation too. Whether it's housing the camera with a more appropriate solution, making sure you have enough battery power to capture a particular event, or needing to see what you're doing from the camera's perspective, these accessories can help accomplish that task.

## Putting your GoPro on a quadcopter

You can fly your GoPro over the landscape, capturing impressive aerial footage with a remote-control device designed for your camera and a quadcopter (see the figure below). A quadcopter uses four rotors to fly where you want it to fly.

**Check your local ordinances before you do this.** The technology is relatively new, and you want to make sure that you don't violate any laws. Violations include flying the quadcopter out of your sight, in a restricted area, or near other flying vehicles.

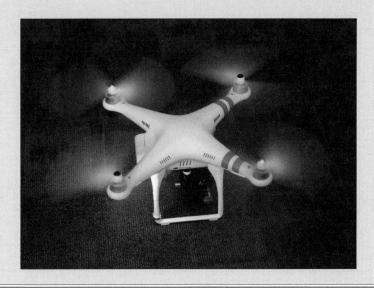

# Part II
# Moviemaking Technique

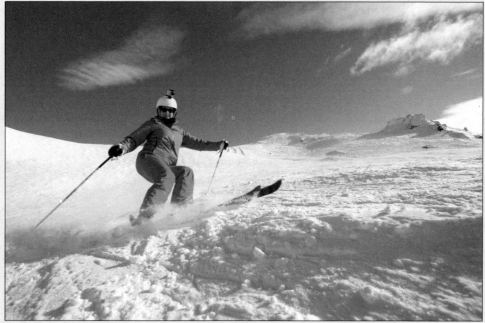

©istockphoto.com/courtneyk Image #45844254

Find out more about mastering your GoPro camera at www.dummies.com/extras/goprocameras.

## *In this part . . .*

- ✔ Use Protune for better control.
- ✔ Explore time-lapse photography.
- ✔ Discover fundamental moviemaking techniques.
- ✔ Master composition techniques.
- ✔ Read the light effectively.
- ✔ Capture the best sound.

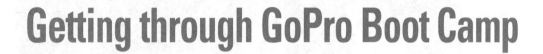

# Getting through GoPro Boot Camp

If you buy a GoPro camera and expect to use it the way you do a video camcorder or a point-and-shoot camera, you quickly find out that this camera doesn't respond well to convention. It's like a beat poet speaking at a 19th-century French literature seminar: Much will get lost in translation. Yet footage captured on a GoPro has been used in all sorts of conventional capacities, from feature films and television shows to sports and news coverage. You just have to understand that it behaves differently from the cameras you're used to using. Sometimes, success begins with putting everything you know on the back burner.

Before you can shoot successfully with your GoPro, however, you have to know how it works. In this chapter, I show you the fundamentals of working with a GoPro.

## Viewing the Lens

If you were playing the "obvious game," the first thing you might say about the GoPro is that the lens is wide (see Figure 4-1). Really wide. A lens this wide is a luxury, and when you realize that it's connected to an affordable camera, it seems more like a luxurious gift.

Yes, this camera offers you boundless creative choices, especially when you're playing with perspective. Still, it's possible to get into trouble with a camera that lacks a viewfinder. Shooting without monitoring the shot isn't much different than drawing in the dark. Both will produce an image, but rarely the way you intended.

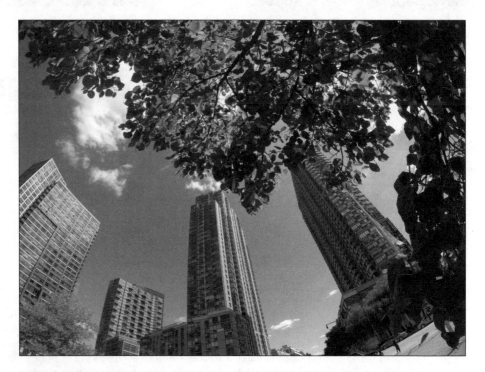

Figure 4-1: The GoPro lets you take unique cityscapes with its ultra-wide-angle lens.

Like everything else, the GoPro's lens has pros and cons. Here are the pros:

- **Fits in tight spaces:** With such a wide angle of view, you can include everything in the shot.
- **Has great depth of field:** The wider the lens, the more of the scene that appears in focus. Because GoPro is really wide, so is the amount of focus in the scene.
- **Gets really close to the subject:** You can use this camera in the tightest of places.

And here are the cons:

- **Records too wide a view:** Sometimes it's possible to "under" lens the scene by having too expansive of a view.
- **Can't control focus:** The camera has no focus control.
- **No viewfinder:** That means you cannot monitor the scene on the camera and therefore judge the view of the lens.
- **Produces geometric warping** (better known as distortion).

## Getting up close and very personal

The GoPro is meant to work in close quarters, so it's most comfortable mere inches from the subject. Thanks to that wide lens, the camera is great for tight, confined areas. Because the field of view is so wide, the sense of depth expands, and objects in the distance appear to be much smaller and farther away. You can position your GoPro inches from the subject and still get a full view. Whether you're capturing a bizarre perspective of a street scene or looking to uniquely show the person in his or her environment, getting close to your subject with this camera provides a fresh look at the world.

Here are some situations that are great for your GoPro:

- ✔ **Shooting in tight spaces:** You can capture almost everything that's in front of the camera, such as a small room, the interior of a stock car, or the inside of an iconic red British phone booth (see Figure 4-2).

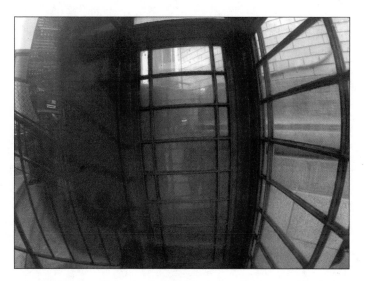

Figure 4-2: Only a couple of feet wide and deep, the interior of this glass phone booth looks downright homey.

- ✔ **Shooting people:** The GoPro is great for scenes showing the subject in his environment. Of course, you'll need to be careful with distortion or he can end up looking like a bobblehead, and not always the good kind.
- ✔ **Capturing street scenes:** The camera matches your periphery of view, so you can capture scenes with both an expansive and personal feel.

✔ **Showing relationships:** Shows relationships in size and distance between objects in the foreground and background.

✔ **Providing an uncommon view of common objects:** Subjects can include geometric shapes, billowy clouds in the sky, and very unusual angles.

## Taking advantage of SuperView

Here's an irony: The GoPro, known for capturing high-definition (HD) and 4K video, actually uses a 4:3 image sensor — a squarish one that resembles the ratio used by old television sets. It's not uncommon for a widescreen camera to use a 4:3 sensor, but it's rare to take advantage of all that space on the sensor.

The GoPro takes advantage of the sensor through its SuperView mode. This new feature combines the best of both worlds by recording the scene with the full sensor vertical resolution of 1440 pixels (p) and then squishing it down to 1080p.

This feature is designed for situations in which you want more vertical resolution than horizontal, such as using the GoPro as a follow or point-of-view camera. The resulting image plays back at a 16:9 ratio but shows more of the scene. The image is slightly unrealistic, as shown in Figure 4-3, mainly because parts of the scene appear to be squished.

Here's what you can expect:

✔ **Immersive wide-angle perspective:** Shows a more inclusive view.

✔ **Distorts shapes:** Makes a round object appear slightly oblong and tall objects slightly shorter.

✔ **Produces more distortion:** Compared with normal 1080p 16:9 video, shows more distortion at the top and bottom of the screen.

## Keeping the lens clean in messy situations

A camera that you can use anywhere — even submerged in water or mud — lets you do a lot of awesome stuff, as Figure 4-4 shows. But although the camera case is waterproof, the lens cover on the waterproof housing isn't self-cleaning like your oven. You have to wipe it constantly; otherwise, many of your cool shots will be taken with goop on the lens.

Here are a few pointers for keeping the lens clean:

✔ **Clean the case, not the lens.** It's much safer and easier to clean the glass on the case than to clean the actual lens. Just use a microfiber cloth and rub gently.

✔ **Don't scrub.** All it takes to scratch the lens is one scrubbed-in speck of dirt. So never scrub the case, let alone the camera lens.

✔ **Wipe the lens housing before you shoot.** Nothing is worse than capturing the greatest footage of your life, only to find that you had dirt on the lens.

✔ **Use a blower brush on the actual lens.** Use a blower brush to clean the camera lens. It's just not worth scratching the lens with a cloth, especially because that scratch will appear in all your movies and images later.

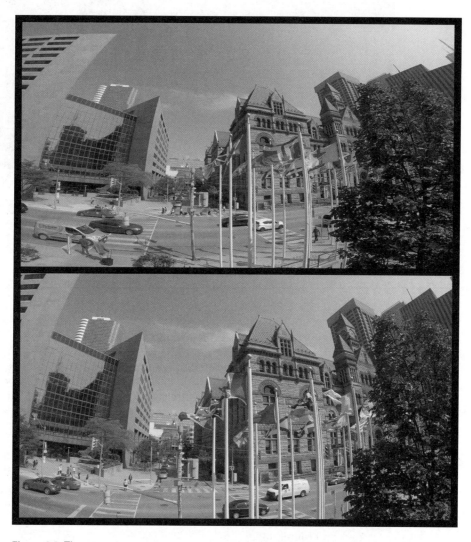

Figure 4-3: The same scene was captured in standard 1080p mode (bottom) and in SuperView mode (top).

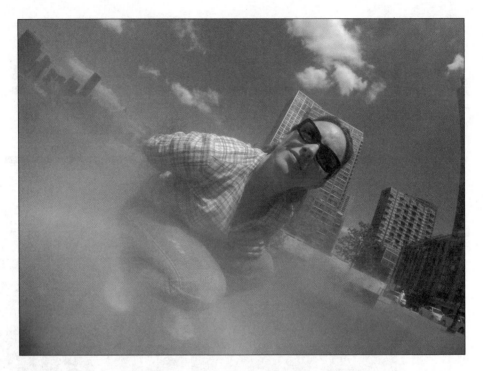

Figure 4-4: While capturing this portrait, I had to keep wiping water off the lens housing.

# Mastering Protune (Hero4, Hero3+ Black Edition)

Although a GoPro camera can do amazing stuff, it still behaves like a point-and-shoot camera. You have little power when it comes to focus and exposure, so you need to live with the footage that the camera captures. Most of the time, the camera renders the scene pretty accurately, but if you're an advanced user looking for a little more control, consider using Protune mode.

Here are some of the benefits of turning it on:

- **High-quality image capture:** When you turn on Protune, the high data increases, so you capture images with less compression, and ultimately better quality.

- **Neutral color:** More accurately, it's flatter to provide flexibility during post-production color correction. It also captures more detail in shadows and highlights.

- **Film/TV frame-rate standard:** Offers more choices for image capture, including the cinema-quality 24 frames per second (fps) setting.

✔ **Compatibility with other effects:** Activating Protune provides more control over camera settings such as resolution and frame rate, which can affect field of view. You can also simultaneously capture video and still images.

## Seeing how it works

Protune puts a little more power in your hands. For one thing, image quality improves because it increases the data rate by more than double. That reduces image compression, thus reducing or eliminating imperfections in the video such as artifacting. Examples of artifacting include jagged edges, showing blocks of pixels, and posterization.

Protune also offers advanced controls. You have a little more control of your footage when you can alter settings such as white balance, exposure, field of view, and color.

In addition, Protune lets you shoot at a more cinema-friendly 24 frames per second (fps). It's not that big a deal for most video shooters, but when you intend to match GoPro footage with other footage captured at 24 fps, such as for a movie, the function is invaluable.

## Enabling Protune on your GoPro

Casual users probably won't want to or need to reap the benefits of Protune. But if you're looking for more quality and better control, you may want to turn it on.

Just follow these steps:

1. **With your GoPro powered up, navigate to the Settings menu.**

   Press the Power/Mode button to cycle through menus until you reach the Settings menu, the one with the wrench icon.

2. **Press the Shutter/Select button to select it.**

3. **Press the Power/Mode button to cycle through settings until you reach Protune.**

4. **Select Protune by pressing the Shutter/Select button.**

   Make sure that the Protune slider is in the on position on the app.

## Setting Protune controls

You can select Protune by going to the Settings menu (the wrench icon) either through the camera or the GoPro App. Protune consists of a group of features that let you fine-tune GoPro capture. Adjusting your Protune settings won't affect non-Protune video modes. You can reset your Protune settings to their default states.

## Camera RAW settings

It's a format that uses minimal processing on the image, so that you can manually apply aspects like color correction, sharpness, saturation, and others to make precise adjustments that meet your specific needs. You need apply these settings in a RAW conversion program, and then export in a file format such as TIFF or JPEG.

Following are some of the powerful settings you can adjust with Protune.

### White balance

You can access this setting through the Protune menu. The icon resembles two triangles looking to catch a small rectangle. White balance adjusts the color temperature between the actual color of the scene and the way your camera records it. By default, white balance on your GoPro is set to Auto, which works pretty well in most situations. If you really want to control the color temperature, however, you can set the white balance manually with several presets (see Figures 4-5 through 4-7):

- ✔ **3000K:** Comes close to the color temperature of indoor lighting.
- ✔ **5500K:** Matches the color of daylight.
- ✔ **6500K:** Matches the tone of an overcast day.
- ✔ **Camera Raw:** Doesn't apply any white-balance setting, so it's pretty much native out of the camera.

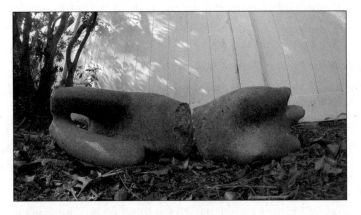

Figure 4-5: Outdoor scene captured with the 3000K setting.

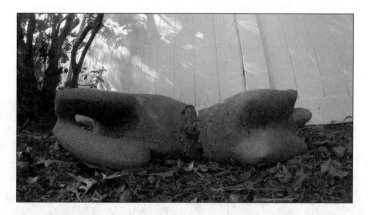

Figure 4-6: Outdoor scene captured with the 5500K setting.

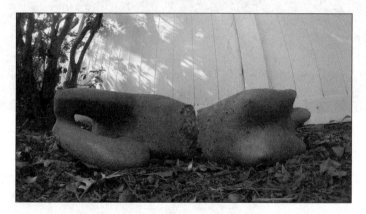

Figure 4-7: Outdoor scene captured with the Camera Raw setting.

### ISO settings

This setting alters the sensitivity of the sensor. For shooting outdoors, you should set the camera to ISO 400, which allows you to adequately capture outdoor scenes with enough light. This setting also captures the scene with the least amount of noise.

When you choose to shoot at dawn or dusk, however, or maybe indoors, you may not have enough light to render the scene properly. To capture a brighter image, you need to bump it up a little bit by increasing the sensitivity of the sensor, which you do by raising the ISO setting. The good news is that you can capture the scene with better exposure. The bad news is that the improved exposure comes at the expense of quality: You'll have noise and grain in the image.

It's a good idea to keep the camera set at the default ISO 400 and make adjustments at those times when you need more light. That way, you can consistently produce clean video. Figure 4-8 and Figure 4-9 show the extremities of this setting.

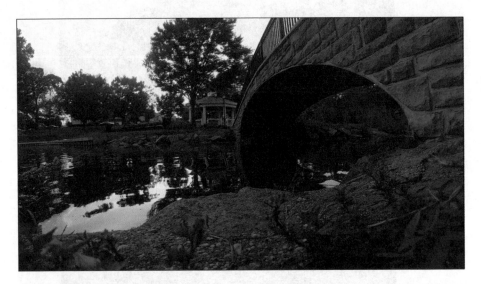

**Figure 4-8:** Under normal lighting conditions at the ISO 400 setting, the scene reproduces with normal color, without much image noise or grain.

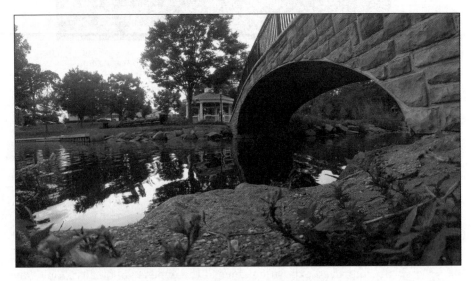

**Figure 4-9:** Shooting the same scene with the ISO 6400 setting adds some noise while slightly mutating the color.

Here are the ISO settings:

- ✔ **400:** The default setting provides the best image quality in normal light conditions. When you use it in lower light levels, your video will be darker than normal.

- ✔ **1600:** Ideal for moderately bright scenes, this setting produces slightly more image noise but is still within acceptable range. Make sure that you set it back to 400 when shooting in bright light.

- ✔ **6400:** Use this setting to capture brighter video in low light (but with increased image noise).

### Sharpness

Like most digital cameras, the GoPro adds digital sharpness after capturing footage to give it the appearance of being sharper. By default, it applies high sharpness to the image, but you can change that setting in Protune to medium or low. The footage will definitely appear softer. You can always enhance it in postproduction, reminiscent of the Camera Raw setting on your DSLR (digital single lens reflex camera). Having control of the footage plays a big part in the look of your movie. You can adjust all these settings on the camera or in the GoPro App on your smartphone (see Figure 4-10).

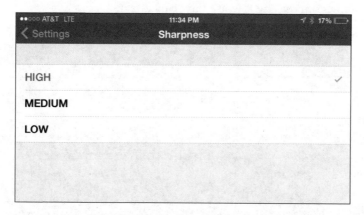

Figure 4-10: Protune lets you control image sharpness and can be accessed through the GoPro App on a smartphone.

You can choose one of three settings:

- ✔ **High:** The default setting applies a great deal of sharpness to the scene. Sometimes it looks fake. That's because sharpness is added (along with other settings) while the image is being processed after you capture it.

✓ **Medium:** This setting is still pretty sharp but provides a bit more realistic appearance to some situations.

✓ **Low:** This setting captures video with the least amount of sharpness but provides the most flexibility in postproduction.

### Color

By default, your camera is set to GoPro Color, which is vibrant and saturated, and makes the video look great. When you're trying to match what you shot on your GoPro with footage captured with another camera, it's a bit harder to match the color.

If you change the setting to Flatter Color, you can do more in postproduction, especially when you're looking to match footage. If not, the GoPro Color setting works pretty well.

### Exposure compensation

Exposure compensation provides a little more control by telling the camera to adjust exposure above or below the normal automatic exposure setting. Figures 4-11, 4-12, and 4-13 show variations in exposure compensation. You can see how greatly they differ. You can adjust brightness only within the existing ISO limit. If brightness has already reached the ISO limit in a low-light environment, increasing it won't have any effect.

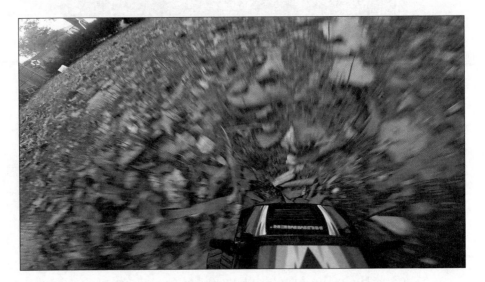

Figure 4-11: GoPro mounted to a radio-controlled car captured with normal exposure.

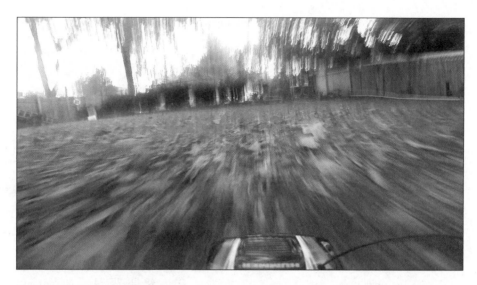

**Figure 4-12:** Captured with the +2.0 exposure compensation setting, the scene appears to be very bright (in photography terms, overexposed).

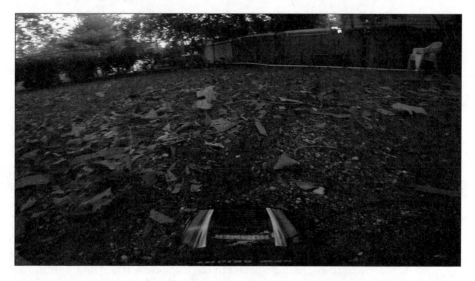

**Figure 4-13:** Captured with the −2.0 exposure compensation setting, the scene is darker than normal (underexposed).

This feature offers the following settings:

| | | |
|---|---|---|
| ✔ +2.0 | ✔ +0.5 | ✔ −1.0 |
| ✔ +1.5 | ✔ +0.0 | ✔ −1.5 |
| ✔ +1.0 | ✔ −0.5 | ✔ −2.0 |

### Resolution

Protune gives you access to more resolutions and frame rates (see Table 4-1).

| Table 4-1 | Non-Protune Resolutions |
|---|---|
| **Resolution** | **Frame Rate (fps)** |
| 4K / 4K (17:9) | 15, 12.5, 12 |
| 2.7K, 2.7K (17:9) | 30, 25, 24 |
| 1440p | 48, 30, 25, 24 |
| 1080p | 60, 50, 48, 30, 25, 24 |
| 1080p (SuperView) | 60, 50, 48, 30, 25, 24 |
| 960p | 100, 60, 50 |
| 720p | 120, 100, 60, 50 |
| 720p (SuperView) | 100, 60, 50 |

## Non-Protune capture settings

Non-Protune settings include the following:

- ✔ **Camera Orientation:** This setting lets you shoot the scene upside down (see Figure 4-14), eliminating the need to rotate the video in post-production. That means you are free to mount the camera and not have to worry about orientation.

- ✔ **Spot Meter:** This setting allows the camera's automatic exposure to base exposure on a much smaller portion of the scene. Use Spot Meter when you're capturing scenes in dark spaces with bright lighting, which can otherwise confuse the automatic exposure setting.

- ✔ **Simultaneous Video and Photo:** This setting lets you simultaneously capture video and still photographs. You can set the camera to take a still image every 5 to 60 seconds while recording video.

  Not all video resolutions support this setting, and you can't use it while Protune is on.

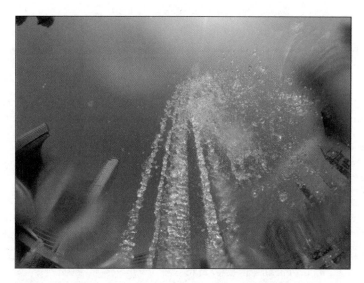

**Figure 4-14:** While you could otherwise hold the camera upside down, or change it in postproduction, there's a fresh perspective when you see it in the monitor upside down while shooting it.

> ✔ **Looping Video:** Like a security camera, this setting continuously records the scene. When space on the memory card runs out, the camera overwrites previously recorded content. You can alter the setting to rerecord after a certain duration (5 to 120 minutes).

Like Simultaneous Video and Photo, this feature doesn't work when Protune is turned on.

## Tooling with Time-Lapse Mode

GoPro is an equal-opportunity camera because it allows you to capture still images that are every bit as impressive as its video. The wide-angle lens provides a crisp, sharp image for pictures that move and the ones that stay perfectly still. The only thing more impressive would be finding a way to mix them. Well, you don't have to look; the time-lapse mode on your GoPro provides the best of both worlds.

### Getting started with time-lapse

A *time-lapse* sequence consists of a bunch of still images that are captured at a constant rate. It's like animation with photographs instead of computer-drawn pictures. By default, time-lapse mode on a GoPro shoots a frame every 0.5 second, but you can capture the scene at intervals as high as 1 frame every 60 seconds.

TECHNICAL STUFF

## Calculating duration

Suppose that you want to create a 30-second time-lapse movie of Thanksgiving dinner with your whole family at the table. You're planning to capture all 2.5 hours from soup to nuts, but you're not quite sure about the duration between frames. If you use a setting of 1 frame per second (fps), for example, your sequence would be around 6 minutes long. Yikes!

The difference between a good time-lapse sequence and a great one often lies in the interval between frames. Striking the proper balance takes a little trial and error. You can select the duration between frames randomly, or you can use a formula.

Instead of guesstimating, use the following formula to calculate exactly how many frames you'll need and the duration between them:

1. **Determine the desired length of the sequence as follows:**

   ```
   (Desired duration in seconds)
      x (Frames per second for playback)
      = Amount of frames for playback.
   ```

A 30-second sequence that plays back at 30 fps would require 900 frames:

```
(30 x 30 = 900)
```

2. **Translate total time into seconds with this formula:**

   ```
   (hours) x (60) x (60) = seconds
   ```

   To record your 2.5-hour family dinner, for example, you'd use the following formula:

   ```
   (2.5 hours) x (60 minutes)
      x (60 seconds) = 9,000 seconds
   ```

3. **Divide the time in seconds (Step 2) by the number of required frames (Step 1) to come up with your frame duration.**

   To make a 30-second movie of your 2.5-hour event, set the digital timer at 1 frame every 12 seconds and then find something to do for the next 2.5 hours.

   ```
   (9,000) / (900) = 10 seconds
   ```

After you capture the sequence, the numerous images are processed in a video editing program (such as GoPro Studio Edit; see Chapter 10) and brought together in order. Sometimes, a time-lapse sequence consists of thousands of images, so you really need an application to put them all together.

### Shooting time-lapse footage

After you power up your GoPro, here's how to record time-lapse footage:

1. **Press the Power/Mode button to cycle through the available modes.**

2. **When you reach Time-Lapse, press the Shutter/Select button to select it.**

   The icon for Time-Lapse mode is a clock next to a camera.

3. **Change the time interval.**

   Go to the Settings menu on the GoPro App and click Time Lapse to find the desired interval.

   The default setting is 0.5 second, but you can capture a frame every 1, 2, 5, 10, 30, or 60 seconds. (For more information, see the nearby sidebar "Calculating duration.")

4. **Press the Shutter/Select button to start time-lapse capture.**

   The camera initiates countdown, and the red status light on front of the camera flashes each time a frame is captured.

5. **Press the Shutter/Select button to stop recording.**

   The red status light flashes three times, and the camera emits three beeps to indicate that time-lapse mode has ended.

## *Making time-lapse easier*

Making time-lapse movies beats a lot of other cool ways to tell a story, but it can be nerve-wracking, too. For one thing, it's a huge time investment. Also, if a glitch occurs, you lose the sequence but gain a few thousand images — not really an equal trade. For that reason, it's important not only to set up the camera properly for time-lapse recording, but to also take a sensible approach to it.

Here are a few pointers:

✔ **Mount it securely.** Whether you opt for a GoPro mount or decide to use a tripod (with the GoPro adapter), be sure that you mount the camera securely. You don't want to introduce motion where it shouldn't exist.

✔ **Take your time.** Plan the shot, and make sure that the subject is properly framed (see Chapter 6). Be on the lookout for elements that can detract from the sequence, such as a bright light or an extraneous object.

✔ **Understand that a time-lapse sequence is a sequence.** Time-lapse recording depends on activity in the frame. Sometimes, that activity is going to be fantastic. At other times, you'll have unpredictable motion in the scene or pedestrians getting too close to the camera, and maybe you'll even catch yourself checking the camera. These moments pose little threat, if any, because they're fleeting and won't be noticed or can be deleted in postproduction (see Part III).

✔ **Use a large, fast memory card.** The card you select should be like a NFL wide receiver: big, strong, and fast. Because time-lapse sequences have the potential to capture a lot of frames at a high resolution, you want a card that has enough capacity to hold them all and enough speed to perform smoothly. Few things are worse than missing key action because you filled the card or the card wasn't fast enough to keep up. A 32MB Class 10 card is ideal (see Chapter 2).

✔ **Have a fully charged battery.** GoPro batteries are notoriously short-lived — battery life is around 2 hours — so it's entirely possible for your camera's battery to drain before the time-lapse sequence ends. Always use a freshly charged battery, and check on the camera often.

✔ **Hurry up and wait.** The name of this process alone — time-lapse — should tip you off that it's quite lengthy. You won't have to do much except wait. You can get some other things done and even walk away from the scene for a while if you'll be nearby.

## Using Other Photo Modes

Besides banging out the occasional still frame and capturing a time-lapse sequence, your GoPro offers more options for capturing still images. You'll notice them when you're scrolling capture modes.

Here are a couple of other photo modes that you may want to check out:

✔ **Continuous:** This mode allows the GoPro to work like a motor drive on a DSLR by capturing 3, 5, or 10 fps for as long as you hold down the Shutter/Select button. Continuous mode is great for capturing action scenes.

✔ **Photo Burst:** This mode acts something like Continuous mode, but it shoots a burst of frames that you set ahead of time. It's great when you want to have a choice of frames in an action sequence. Figure 4-15 shows a few of the frames that were in the capture using the burst mode; Figure 4-16 shows the perfect one.

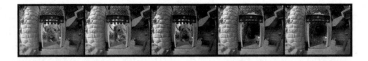

Figure 4-15: Photo Burst mode. The burst was set to capture 30 frames in 3 seconds. This illustration shows five frames.

You can use one of the following settings:

• 3 photos in 1 second

• 5 photos in 1 second

- 10 photos in 1 second
- 10 photos in 2 seconds
- 30 photos in 1 second
- 30 photos in 2 seconds
- 30 photos in 3 seconds

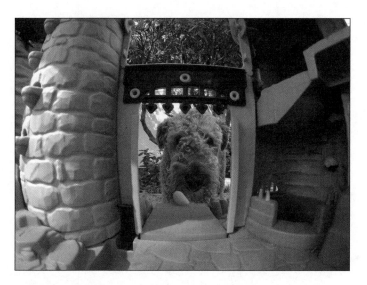

**Figure 4-16:** There's a monster at the castle door! This frame shows the dog just noticing the carrot before devouring it.

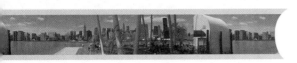
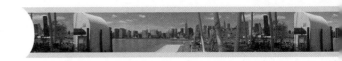

# 5

# Understanding Effective Camera Techniques

............................................

## In This Chapter

▷ Focusing on the camera's fundamentals

▷ Shooting effectively

............................................

*T*he camera's size is the first thing that lets you know that making a movie with a GoPro is very different from using any other camera. After all, not many serious cameras resemble an accessory for your niece's favorite American Girl doll. But don't judge a book by its cover or a camera by its proportions. This formidable camera holds its own despite its diminutive appearance.

Regardless of your expertise in making movies or taking photographs, getting the most out of your GoPro requires a fresh approach, because GoPro shooting is a novel experience. You have limited control of exposure, focus, and focal length, for example, which makes it important to find the best places to mount the camera and compose the scene effectively.

In this chapter, I show you how to devote your time and energy to making a great GoPro movie.

## Nailing GoPro Fundamentals

Proper planning is the key to success with a GoPro. It takes a few extra moments to make sure that the composition, color, and light are all right for the shot, but staying aware of how you capture each scene strengthens the final appearance of the movie. That's how the pros do things.

## Understanding the camera's limitations

Unlike the camcorder or DSLR (digital single lens reflex camera) you may be comfortable using, the GoPro offers far fewer controls. It handles most of the technical settings automatically, and the focal length is limited to a single angle of view (albeit very wide-angle). The Black Edition offers some variations by providing a narrow and medium angle of view. Basically, it shoots the scene at a higher resolution setting and crops it to fit the frame, so there is no loss of quality. The 2.7K mode provides enough resolution for the medium view; the 4K mode allows you to capture a narrower section.

So when you're on a lonely, desolate stretch of highway, a single-pump gas station has all that you need. A GoPro isn't much different. The camera is simple to operate, leaving the creative stuff up to you. That "creative stuff" includes setting up the camera properly, arranging each shot effectively, and solving each problem that pops up. Every time something changes in the scene or you move the camera, it's important to make adjustments.

In many ways, not having to focus or set exposure is some of the camera's greatest assets. Still, you'll need to find ways to work around (or to work with) the following limitations of the GoPro:

✔ **No adjustable aperture setting:** The *aperture setting* determines the amount of light that goes into the lens. GoPro sets it automatically. With another camera, you might adjust the aperture setting to increase or decrease depth of the focus in a scene, but you don't have that option when you're working with an ultra-wide-angle lens.

✔ **No adjustable shutter speed:** Depending on the subject, lighting, and level of action, adjusting the shutter speed offers a little more control. Slow speeds produce blurred images; higher ones can capture crisp action. GoPro doesn't allow you to change the shutter speed, but it does offer a wide range of frame rates, which you *can* adjust to achieve the same effects.

✔ **No manual focus:** You don't have much to focus with a lens that covers a 170-degree angle of view. Just about anything in the scene is in focus as long as it's more than a few inches away (see Figure 5-1).

## The GoPro isn't a point-and-shoot camera

Recently, I overheard someone comparing the GoPro with a point-and-shoot camera. Although the camera's manual controls are somewhat limited, it's more than a point-and-shoot.

Still, the term is misleading for referring to automatic cameras. Even the most expensive DSLR can be used in a fully automatic mode. So while GoPro limits your control over exposure and focal length, if it's a point-and-shoot camera then it's one on steroids. Great movies are always made by hand, so be more concerned with setting up the shot and less about the automatic stuff.

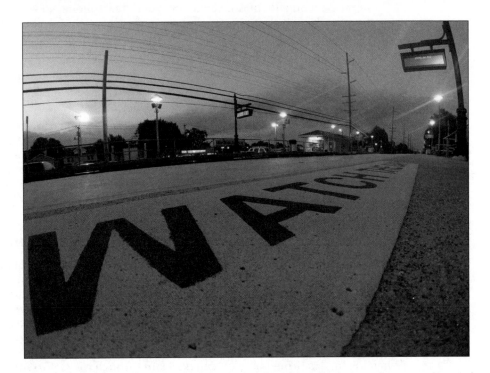

Figure 5-1: Though the GoPro is only a few inches from this reflective warning on a train platform, the entire picture is in focus.

## *Checking your setup*

"Measure twice, cut once" works for moviemakers as well as carpenters. Taking a little extra time to make sure that everything is set right goes a long way. Making sure that a shot is technically perfect means double-checking the monitor, ensuring that the mount is secure, and verifying that the camera is set properly.

## Getting exposure just right

It's a tall order when you need to figure out how to fine-tune exposure with a camera that offers no manual settings, but GoPro moviemaking requires a different way of thinking. You can still control image quality, but the process is different from changing the aperture or lowering the shutter speed.

Here are some pointers:

- **Monitor the scene with your GoPro App.** Because most of the time you will be nowhere near your GoPro, it's necessary to monitor the scene so you can compose it properly and check the exposure. You probably already spend a lot of time checking your smartphone, so why not use it to check each shot on your GoPro, too? (I cover the app in detail in Chapter 6.)

- **Use exposure compensation.** Exposure compensation is the next-best thing to setting exposure manually. This feature (activated when you turn on Protune; see Chapter 4) lets you increase or decrease the automatic exposure setting a few steps.

- **Set your ISO manually.** Depending on the situation, you can alter the camera's ISO setting to capture bright or dimly lit scenes properly. A bright daylight scene does well when you set the camera at ISO 400, for example; for a low-light situation such as a night scene or a dark club, try using ISO 6400 to increase sensor sensitivity. As with exposure compensation, you must enable Protune to change ISO settings manually.

## Maintaining accurate color (models with Protune)

The GoPro normally reproduces a scene with punchy, saturated color. That setting works well for many situations, but on some occasions, you want to fine-tune color or take a more stylized approach. Maybe you want to use color temperature to convey a feeling in the scene. A warmly lit scene may evoke coziness, whereas a cool blue rendering evokes distance and isolation or tells the viewer, "Hey, it's pretty cold here."

When Protune is turned on, you can navigate through the GoPro App to the Color setting to adjust the color profile of your video footage. Here are the settings:

- **GoPro Color:** The default color setting, providing user with the color profile they know and love.

- **Flat:** Provides a neutral color profile that captures more shadows and highlights. Uncorrected, this setting doesn't look very appealing, as seen in Figure 5-2, but it provides the most flexibility when it comes to postproduction. Figure 5-3 shows corrected color.

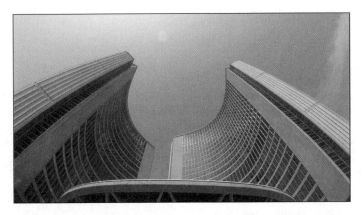

Figure 5-2: The color is pretty dull.

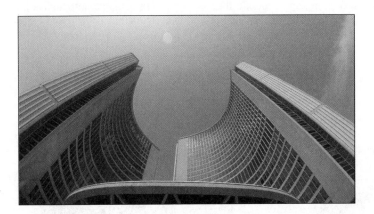

Figure 5-3: The image looks much better.

## Keeping the camera steady

Although technical settings contribute to the success of each shot, none of them matters much if you can't keep the camera steady. Camera stability is an important part of the equation, like following your grandmother's recipe for reindeer cookies.

Make sure that the camera remains steady throughout your shots. GoPro offers more mounting accessories than an equestrian boutique (see Chapter 3), so choose the right mount for the job to make sure that the camera is secure. Also, check that everything is tightened properly. If you mount a GoPro on your skateboard, and the thumbscrew on the mount is loose, the resulting footage will show the camera slipping.

# Using the camera on a tripod

For general image stability, nothing beats a tripod. Using a tripod with your GoPro requires the accessory tripod mount (see Chapter 3), which serves as an adapter between the camera and the tripod head. If you opt to use one for your next GoPro capture, try the following tips:

- **Place the tripod on level ground.** Make sure that you plant the tripod firmly on a level surface.

- **Check that everything is tightened.** This includes the GoPro mount.

- **Keep an eye on the horizon.** Because the camera has such a wide view, any slight movement of the mount will make the footage look as though like the world is sliding downhill. Unless you have a specific creative purpose in mind, an evenly balanced horizon is essential. Be sure to monitor the scene in the GoPro App on your smartphone before pressing the Shutter/Select button.

- **Position the tripod properly.** Chances are that you'll be close to the subject, so if you're using a standard tripod, try *not* to point one of the tripod legs toward the subject. Otherwise, you risk getting the tripod leg in the shot or causing someone trip to over it. If you're using something like a GorillaPod, make sure that it's wrapped securely around whatever you wrap it around.

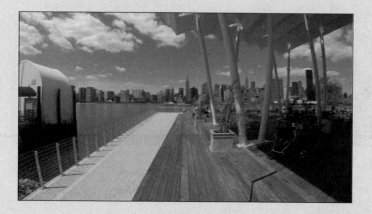

At one point or another, you may consider holding the camera in one hand and your smartphone (running the GoPro App) in the other. Don't even think about hitting the wet stuff with your GoPro with smartphone in tow. It's like going out with Superman and finding that bullets don't bounce off your chest.

## Keeping your fingers out of the shot

More than likely, you won't be holding your GoPro, but that doesn't mean you won't get your digits in the frame every now and again (see Figure 5-4). This is bound to happen sometimes, because the camera has no viewfinder and a very wide-angle lens. Be extra careful to keep your fingers out of the shot.

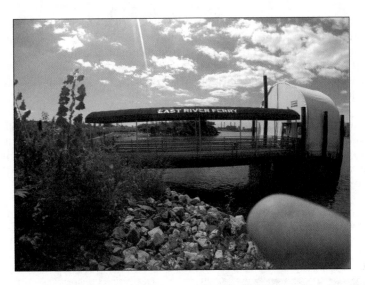

Figure 5-4: My finger has a walk-on role in this shot.

# Shooting Your Movie

The success of your movie depends heavily on how effectively you capture each scene, and part of that process involves shooting enough variations of each scene. Having several angles and perspectives to choose among helps you alter the movie's visual rhythm and give it a nice flow.

Deviations within shots make for powerful editing and help you pace the movie. It's not unusual for a movie to have a 20:1 ratio (or greater) of shots captured to shots used.

But not being stingy about shooting variations of each shot doesn't give you license to overshoot. If you do, you'll spend too much time going through the footage and second-guessing what you included in the edit and what you put on the storyboard.

## Finding the best position for the camera

There's a certain swagger to GoPro movies that makes them stand out from their more conventional counterparts. Whether it's a segment of breathtaking action sequences, unique perspectives, or a little of both, there's something truly distinctive about movies made with this camera. But they're not impervious to the fundamentals of the best places to put the camera.

That's because great moviemaking revolves around assembling an array of shots that comes together like a visual symphony. If you think of each shot as a note of music, you will realize that sometimes it doesn't matter how beautiful that note sounds on its own, because it needs other notes for it to sound complete. The same thing happens when you apply a nice mix of shots to your movie.

So variety isn't just the spice of life, it also adds flavor to your movie. That means altering the camera-to-subject distance or mixing in different angles keeps the viewer more interested in your movie than, say, using a bunch of eye-level shots. Don't get me wrong — they're necessary, but if that's all you got, your audience will suffer from terminal yawning.

It also means putting the camera in unusual places to show a unique view, such as using a roll bar mount to attach the camera on a shovel, as seen in Figure 5-5.

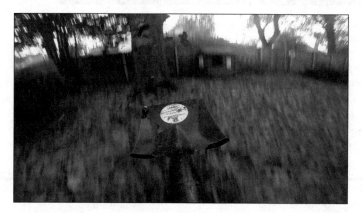

Figure 5-5: Attaching the camera to a shovel handle during fall leaf cleanup shows an interesting perspective.

## Shooting to edit

Rather than shoot everything that happens in front of the camera, it's more effective to shoot to edit. Shooting to edit means having an idea about the structure of the movie — or the number of scenes you want to include — and then creating each scene with three or more variations. The simplest form of shooting to edit means getting a wide-angle, normal, and close-up view of each subject.

Shooting to edit is a little more complicated with the GoPro, however, because its fixed lens covers a very wide angle of view, making normal view hard and zoom impossible.

Here are some options for varying your shots:

- **Shoot variations of each shot in the scene.** At the very least, include variations to subject size and angle. This makes it easier to choose shots in the editing process.

- **Change the Field of View.** Altering the size of the subject in the frame provides de facto versions of wide, close-up, and normal views.

- **Shoot at different angles.** Besides shooting at eye level, place the camera high and shoot down on the subject, or mount the camera low and shoot up at the subject.

- **Alter the composition.** You have a lot of frame to play with, so use it to your advantage by incorporating various compositional devices such as the rule of thirds, subject placement, and framing (see Figure 5-6). For a more thorough list of compositional choices, take a look at Chapter 6.

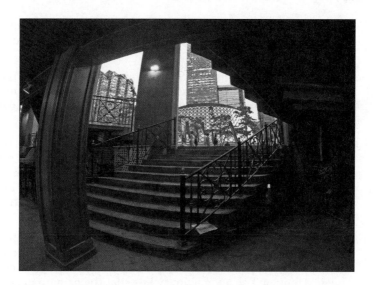

Figure 5-6: Framing the subject provides a nice option for your edit.

## Alternating shots, GoPro style

GoPro uses a single focal length to make movies, but that's not so unusual. Often, feature films are shot with a single lens. Changing the camera-to-subject distance and perspective varies shots. But the big difference is that cinema cameras generally use a lens with a normal perspective. In the 35mm world, that would be the 50mm normal lens. Its perspective lies between being slightly wide and slightly telephoto.

GoPro makes alternating shots a little more challenging because it's just wide. It's still possible to get a good variation of shots with your GoPro; you just need to get a bit creative.

## Maintaining continuity between shots

Most films are shot out of sequence and put together in postproduction like a giant puzzle. Sometimes when the movie is being assembled, though, a scene may be compromised because something changed from shot to shot. Maybe that can of soda that was on the edge of the counter in one shot is on the other side in another shot. Or maybe the actor's shirt was buttoned differently in a couple of shot. Isolating all the details makes for logistical nightmares. Many mistakes are so minor that audiences wouldn't even notice them. But that doesn't mean you shouldn't be as careful as possible.

These pointers can prevent problems in your movie:

- **Keep a detailed record of each scene.** The proof is in the picture. The better your recollection of a scene, the better your chances of ordering other shots properly.

- **Keep the action plausible.** Successful editing thrives on the rhythm between shots, so it's necessary they remain plausible. Don't show a sequence of someone getting into a car, and then showing it moving in the opposite direction because the light was better.

- **Watch the subject's primary movements.** Sometimes it's hard with this camera, especially when shooting action. Regardless, be sure the subject's actions remain consistent. For example, if the subject has his right hand raised slightly in the wide shot, then make sure it's not lowered in the medium shot. These minor breeches can still break the suspension of disbelief in your movie, so be aware of them.

- **Try not to break the 180-degree rule.** This establishes the screen direction of the action. It's the same premise as a stage production, where everything happens in front of the audience, or within their peripheral view. Think of it as an imaginary line that the camera must stay behind in order to maintain continuity. Easier said than done with a GoPro, but many continuity problems occur when the succeeding shot does not maintain the periphery of human vision.

## When to stop and start the camera

When to stop and start the camera is actually a practical question. You can't peek through a viewfinder on most models and press the shutter at the right moment. Nor can you fully trust the GoPro App on your smartphone because it has a two-second delay. So here's some advice on when to stop and start:

✓ **Use the GoPro App on your smartphone:** Whenever possible, this provides the best way to record each scene, even with the two-second delay. Not only can you look at the shot, but also you don't have to touch the camera, possibly overturning it. You can control up to 50 cameras. You can also use the GoPro remote.

✓ **Start early:** No matter what kind of camera you're using, it's always best to pre-roll so that the action begins after you started recording. The same applies for stopping the record. Let it breathe a bit before ending the record.

✓ **Use the burst mode for stills:** You can alter its setting to how many frames it captures as well as the duration. For moving scenes that you don't want to miss, set the camera on burst and press the Shutter/Select button. You can always discard the outtakes.

---

# Using multiple GoPros

You can control up to 50 cameras with the GoPro remote control, starting and stopping them remotely. Here are a few reasons to use more than one GoPro for a shoot:

✓ **Extreme action:** Extreme action is the kind of thing you want to capture from different perspectives because you don't know whether you're going to be able to get it again.

✓ **Shoot multiple angles simultaneously:** Filmmakers rarely shoot with multiple cameras because it's too expensive. But when a camera capable of 4K capture costs less to own than a one-day rental of a camcorder, the choice is a no-brainer.

✓ **3D moviemaking:** GoPro makes it easy to make a 3D movie. All you need are a second camera and the DualHero System. That's the tandem housing used for capturing 3D movies. The rest, you can put together in GoPro Studio Edit (see Chapter 10).

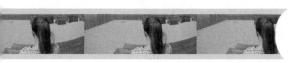

# 6

# Framing the Shot

• • • • • • • • • • • • • • • • • • • • • • • • • • • • • • • • • • • • • • • • • • • • • •

## *In This Chapter*

▶ Understanding the elements of visual style

▶ Composing the scene

▶ Putting the camera in the perfect place

▶ Using the GoPro App while you shoot

▶ Giving yourself options

• • • • • • • • • • • • • • • • • • • • • • • • • • • • • • • • • • • • • • • • • • • • • •

*G*reat films are built on the creative use of visual elements such as composition, camera angle, color, and lighting. The GoPro adds its own
perspective to the mix, thanks to its fixed wide-angle view and its capability
to go almost anyplace.

Although the GoPro is a relatively new concept, shooting with
an ultra-wide-angle lens is not. Some professional directors
rely on it for an occasional shot; others swear by it. Terry
Gilliam (director and founding member of the British
sketch-comedy group Monty Python) shoots nearly all
of his films with a rectilinear wide-angle lens, which
gives his films a unique look.

What Gilliam does is what we're all looking to do:
differentiating ourselves from the pack through
our special way of seeing a story. Finding your own
visual style begins by understanding the fundamentals. That's what will make you different from your
cousin Jim or your former college roommate who also
has a GoPro. The ultimate goal is to find your visual
style and build on it.

This chapter shows you how to use classic visual elements to
create a compelling film — GoPro style.

# Understanding Time-Honored Visual Basics

Here's a pretty cool saying about composition: "What happens in the frame stays in the frame." More accurately, what happens in the frame is all that people can see. Take the time to provide essential visual content, but do it economically enough that you don't clutter the frame.

How you choose to occupy the frame plays a big part in the success of your movie. No matter what technology you use, what happens in each shot stands on its own but also influences other shot. Not sure what I'm talking about? Check out the shower scene in Alfred Hitchcock's classic thriller *Psycho* or the "Here's Johnny" close-up of Jack Nicholson in *The Shining*. There's nothing random about these shots; they were strategically arranged. The directors understood how to fill the frame.

Creating an effective composition has its challenges, especially with a camera that captures the world with an ultra-wide angle view. But that doesn't mean you can't find a happy medium. Besides, each of us sees the world a little differently, so here's a breakdown of the components of visual technique.

## Proper composition

As in Fight Club, the first rule of composition is that there are no rules. Composition is about understanding how to fill the frame in a way that effectively and efficiently communicates your intention to the viewer. There's psychology behind arrangement of scenes. Normally, people look from left to right and top to bottom. That mechanism works for reading and for effectively arranging a scene to capture video or a still frame.

Here are two examples of how a viewer can interpret a scene, based on the way it's arranged:

- **Positioning the subject at bottom right:** This arrangement draws viewers to the subject (see Figure 6-1) as they look across and down at the frame.

- **Positioning the subject at top left:** When the subject is in the top-left corner of the frame (see Figure 6-2), the viewer can share the perspective of the subject in the scene.

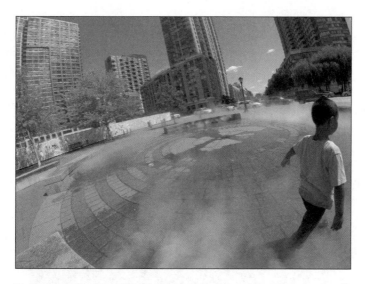

Figure 6-1: When the subject is in the bottom-right corner, the viewer's eye follows him.

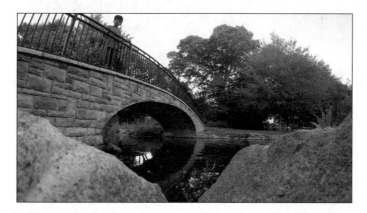

Figure 6-2: Subject at top left.

## Coherent shot arrangement

Basic shot structure with a GoPro differs somewhat from the approach you would take with a conventional camcorder or DSLR (digital single lens reflex camera). The GoPro uses a fixed wide-angle lens, whereas the others use a zoom lens that covers lots of focal lengths (but nowhere as wide as the lengths that the GoPro's lens can cover).

Instead of using focal length to bring a shot in tight, control the variations in the size of the subject in the frame solely with camera-to-subject distance. Typical shot arrangements such as wide, medium, and close-up take on different meanings with the GoPro. If you're using the Black Edition, it's possible to change the Field of View. Here are some of the shots you can get:

- ✔ **Ultra-wide:** This shot covers a wide area of the scene with nothing looking as though it's anywhere near the camera (see Figure 6-3).

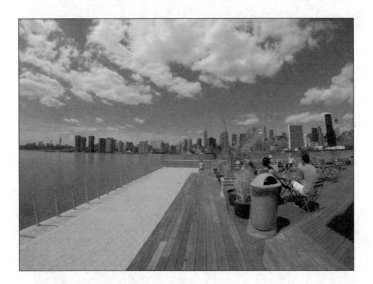

Figure 6-3: Normal ultra-wide GoPro view.

- ✔ **Very wide:** This shot still covers an expansive area, but some objects appear to be closer (see Figure 6-4).

- ✔ **Fairly wide:** Objects in the scene are much closer to the lens, though not that close that the ultra-wide angle view makes them seem a little distant. Meanwhile the subject is probably only a few feet away, as seen in Figure 6-5.

- ✔ **Intimate wide:** This shot is still wide but fills the frame with the subject, who may be just inches away (see Figure 6-6). Think of this view as being the GoPro's version of a close-up.

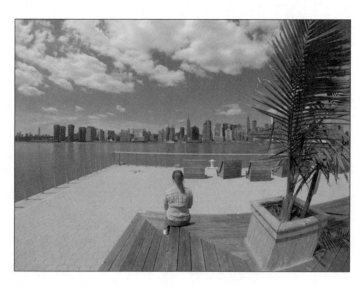

**Figure 6-4:** Expansive GoPro view.

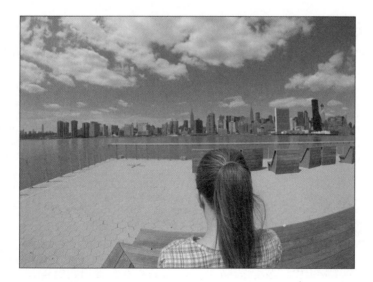

**Figure 6-5:** Wide GoPro view.

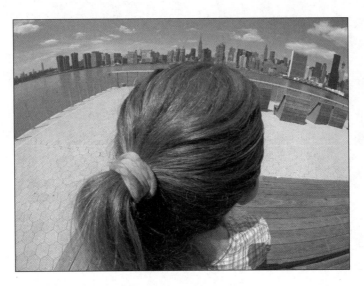

Figure 6-6: A shot taken right next to the subject.

# Breaking Down Shot Lingo

Great filmmaking weaves different shot types throughout a story. The different sizes at which you depict a subject in the frame help create a visual narrative.

Here's an in-depth description of various shot types:

- **Long shot:** Some people call this shot an extreme wide-angle shot, but I call it the result of using your GoPro like a conventional camera. This expansive shot establishes an overall view of the setting and is often used as the first shot in the edit. It's not always necessary to include actors; a wide landscape with few identifiable subjects qualifies for this type of shot.

- **Very wide shot:** This shot isn't as expansive as a long shot but is still pretty wide. It can also work as an establishing shot.

- **Wide shot:** In the wide world of wide shots, this shot isn't really that wide. It works well with people, presenting them from head to toe. Frequently, this shot is used to set up medium and close-up shots.

- **Medium or normal shot:** This shot takes a more distinct view of the subject, showing more of him than in a wide shot and much less than in a close-up — perhaps from the waist up. If you shoot from a higher angle, you can make the subject look like a bobblehead doll, with his head being much larger than the rest of his body.

- **Two shot:** This shot shows interaction between two subjects: a conversation or confrontation. Sometimes, the subjects are shown full-figure; at other times, they're shown from the waist up.

✓ **Medium close-up:** One way to think of it is as the close-up for people who don't like close-ups. This shot captures a person's entire face, with a little bit of her neck and chest. If the subject is an object instead of the person, the object can loosely fill the frame. Often, this shot is the closest you're going to get to a subject with a GoPro without totally distorting that subject.

✓ **Close-up:** This shot is pretty close, and some people may not like you coming this close. The frame shows the subject from the neck up. It shows the head, hair, and face but not pores and blemishes.

✓ **Extreme close-up:** This shot shows lots of detail on inanimate objects, but you may get hit with an object if you try to use this shot on a human with your GoPro.

✓ **Point of view:** This shot shows the scene as the subject sees it (see Figure 6-7) and makes for a great selection of shots for editing. Many GoPro mounts help you achieve this type of shot; see Chapter 3 for a few examples.

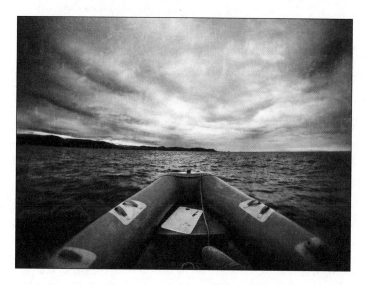

©istockphoto.com/piola666 Image #37074252

**Figure 6-7:** Point-of-view shot.

✓ **Cutaway:** All sorts of productions, from news broadcasts and documentaries to feature films and reality television programs, use this device. Generally, it has little to do with the story; it merely helps set the scene.

✓ **Cut in:** This shot shows details such as the subject's cracking his knuckles, picking up a glass, or tapping his fingers.

## Take some tips from the movies

The next time you're watching a movie, analyze the shot structure. Feature films include the following shots:

- **Establishing shot:** Generally, this shot is a wide-angle shot that lets the viewer get a sense of the landscape, place, or logistics of a scene. An establishing shot usually is the opening shot of a movie, but it can also depict location or time changes.

- **Wide:** A wide shot is an expansive view of the scene that shows the subject in relation to his or her environment.

- **Medium:** A medium shot is an average perspective, not too close and not too far. It's excellent for shots that include dialogue.

- **Close-up:** A close-up is a magnified view of a scene. Sometimes, it brings distant objects closer or emphasizes important details.

- **Pan:** A pan is a sweeping motion over a scene, from side to side.

- **Tilt:** A tilt is the camera's way of looking up, down, or up and down.

- **Tracking shot:** A tracking shot uses focal length to draw the subject closer or farther away in a scene.

## Following Simple Framing Rules

Cinematic composition can follow the same time-honored rules as traditional pictorial composition. The following sections present some of the most prominent rules of composition.

### Observe the rule of thirds

Have you ever wondered why Greek architecture remains aesthetically pleasing more than 2,000 years later? The reason is the Greeks' time-honored approach of balancing a shape in thirds — an approach that they called the Golden Mean. Today, we call this approach the *rule of thirds*.

Here are a few guidelines:

- **Don't place the main subject dead center.** Imagine the frame divided into three parts — horizontal, vertical, and center — with the center being off limits to the subject (see Figure 6-8).

- **Lead the viewer.** It's your choice to lead the view into or out of the frame. Remember, the earlier discussion of positioning the subject.

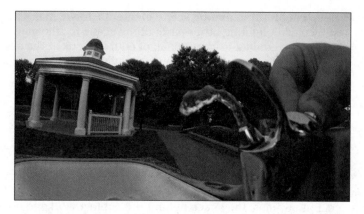

Figure 6-8: Following the rule of thirds, nothing is in the center of the frame.

- **Be mindful of the horizon.** Placing the horizon line in the center of the frame is almost as boring as placing the subject in the middle. Instead, place the horizon on one of the dividing lines to show more sky or foreground. Make sure that the GoPro is level; otherwise, the shot will have image distortion because of its wide-angle lens.
- **Mind your subject's head.** Always have a little room to avoid giving your subject a flat top.

## Keep things simple

Although the axiom "Less is more" can apply to many things, in filmmaking, it refers to including only pertinent visual information. When you keep the scene free of extraneous clutter, the viewer immediately recognizes the center of interest and doesn't have to take a moment to figure it out. Sounds easy, right? Not all the time. Sometimes, you don't notice clutter in the frame until you start editing. Before pressing the Shutter/Select button, make sure that the shot is concise and that the viewer clearly understands the center of interest.

Keep in mind the following guidelines:

- **Avoid complicated backgrounds.** A complicated background features a laundry list of elements that can range from objects strewn behind the subject to a light ratio beyond what the camera can handle. Recompose the scene if the sky is too bright or if a telephone pole appears to be growing out of the subject's head.
- **Focus on simplicity.** When a scene concentrates on the subject, try framing the subject against a plain background, even if the scene takes place in a busy area.

✓ **Keep competition among scene elements down.** Make sure that the subject isn't fighting other parts of the scene for the viewer's attention — unless the conflict is intentional, of course. Look at the scene through the viewer's eyes; see whether you understand what the subject is.

✓ **Track the shot efficiently.** If the camera follows the subject, be sure that it doesn't lead the viewer into a heap of clutter. Tracking the subject in an open field that leads to a cluster of telephone wires would be leading the viewer into clutter. Recompose the scene if necessary.

## Take advantage of the background

Not placing the subject against a complicated background qualifies as good advice. But at times, the space behind the subject works to your advantage. Colorful, simple, or picturesque backgrounds fall into this category and can even enhance the quality of the scene.

The human eye can effectively distinguish elements in a scene thanks to depth perception, but the camera can't. A movie frame is two-dimensional, so sometimes it can't differentiate screen elements properly. Because the GoPro has such a wide lens, almost the entire scene is in focus, so discrepancies between the foreground and background can blend together.

When dealing with backgrounds with your GoPro, consider the following:

✓ **Keep an eye on vertical lines.** Be sure that telephone poles, trees, street lamps, and other sticklike objects don't converge with the subject. These objects can appear to be unusual appendages or look like part of a shish kabob.

✓ **Understand that the scene is two-dimensional.** Movies and photographs appear to be compressed, mainly because humans see the world as 3D, but the camera renders it as 2D.

✓ **Complement the subject.** Let the background work for the subject. The interview in your skateboarding movie, for example, should have something going on in the skateboard park behind the subject, such as someone doing a halfpipe. In a skydiving movie, a plane or hanger could complement the subject.

## Put people first

Whether you're posing the subject against a background or capturing yourself in an action scene, follow these guidelines:

✓ **Determine whether the subject should look into the camera.** Whether the subject is you or someone else, decide whether the subject is going to talk to the audience. Generally, in an interview, the subject shouldn't look into the camera. But if you're filming a first-person account of some event, it's completely acceptable for the subject to look at the camera.

- **Don't ignore the basics.** Follow the rule of thirds (see "Observe the rule of thirds" earlier in this chapter) for subject placement in the frame. Avoid putting the subject in the center. Also, keep an eye on the background.

- **Find a flattering angle.** Because the GoPro has a nearly fish-eye view, the difference between a subject's looking like a man and looking like fish may be a matter of a few inches.

## Use shadows and reflections wisely

Shadows and reflections not only look good onscreen, but also help unify a scene, especially when it includes a one-sided arrangement. Including shadows in the frame can provide a sense of depth, warning, or foreboding. Reflected images (see Figure 6-9) tend to grab viewers' attention, especially when they involve rich textures. Sometimes capturing shadows and reflections also works as the main subject.

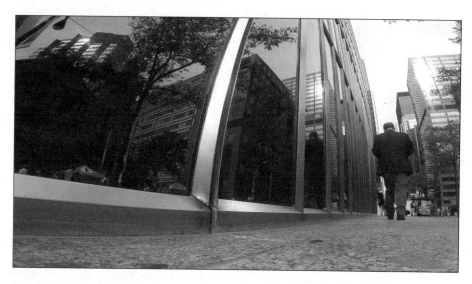

Figure 6-9: Reflected image.

Balancing the frame with a shadow or reflection serves many purposes. It can make a statement about the scene, such as the time of day, or it can make a nice selection for your shot arrangement. Also, it makes a drab subject look more interesting.

## Other composition devices

If you follow the rule of thirds and watch the background each time you record, you probably don't need to worry about much else. When you decide to add more visual magic, however, you have a couple more visual devices to consider:

- **Sweeping curve:** Lead the viewer on a sweeping diagonal journey from the top of the frame to the bottom, or vice versa. This technique works best when the scene is shot from overhead, because it leads the viewer on a visual journey.

- **Shape and form:** Sometimes, it's effective to depict the subject as a shape or form. Viewers are attracted to geometric patterns.

Here are some things to consider about using shadows and reflections in your shots:

- Treat a shadow like any other subject, either by including it in its entirety or by defining a segment (shape, form, or feature).

- If the shadow or reflection is the center of interest, focus attention on it instead of the subject.

- Be careful not to get a reflection of your GoPro in the shot, and make sure that the light behind the camera doesn't create a shadow.

## Art-Directing the Scene

In this section, I present more advanced approaches to unifying your vision for the movie.

### Arranging elements in the scene

It's a bit deceptive to say that you're arranging elements in the scene when you're actually positioning the camera to include, omit, or capture the subject at a specific angle within the context of the frame. Because the GoPro has an incredibly wide-angle view, sometimes it's challenging to compose a scene.

It's visually effective to position the camera as close to the subject as possible for an intimate view. Using foreground objects to frame the scene works well as another creative device that makes for an interesting shot. Whether you're capturing a doorway, archway, tree branch, peephole, or just about anything else on the periphery of the shot, this technique can define the center of interest in the frame.

## Making the GoPro's view work for you

Thanks to the camera's super-wide 170-degree view, it's best to think of each scene you shoot with your GoPro as having a foreground, middle ground, and background. By paying attention to all three elements, you'll be able to follow basic cinematic principles, and before long, the limitations of focal length will become an asset.

Here are a few pointers:

- **Maintain attention on the subject.** Don't worry if the framing elements are out of focus, as in Figure 6-10. Besides, when you're capturing such a wide view, it's unlikely much of the scene will be out of focus.

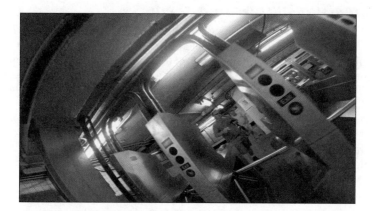

Figure 6-10: Framing the shot.

- **Frame the people too.** If you frame the main subject with people in the shot, it's best to have the people look into the center of the frame, as opposed to out of it. This technique affects the audience's view of what's important; that view is based on where the people onscreen are looking.

- **Don't place the subject on the edge of the frame.** While dead center is often boring place for the subject, the GoPro's wide angle view can severely distort it.

## Keeping things in balance

Balancing elements such as color, shape, and light in the frame creates a legitimate order in which the viewer can process the scene. Another method places subject matter on both sides to form an even composition. In this sort of arrangement, it's acceptable to put the subject in the center.

Then there's asymmetrical balance, in which the subject shares the frame with negative or blank space to depict vastness or difference. Also, the juxtaposition of color is another means of making the scene look interesting. You can position a warmly lit subject against a cool blue backdrop, for example. Complementary colors are described as the opposite pairs of colors that produce the strongest contrast to one another. Here are a few colors and their complementary colors:

- Green/magenta
- Red/cyan
- Blue/yellow

## Creating subtext in a scene

There are many definitions of subtext in film, but one of the most common ways of showing it is called mise-en-scène (a French term that translates to "placing on stage"). Mise-en-scène occurs when everything comes together in the frame to convey the intention of a scene. Essentially, it's a poetic way of visually conveying what you want the audience to take from the scene.

This message comes together in a variety of ways, mostly through the decor of the set, the arrangement of elements, and the lighting. Sometimes, it's created in the editing process. One example is cutting away to a locomotive blowing its whistle when the subject begins to show anger.

Here are a few other ways to get this message across to your viewer.

- Use cool blue lighting to depict the subject's despair.
- Having the subject look up to the sky after a confrontation may suggest that he's looking for guidance.
- Having the subject take a walk early in the morning can alert the audience to the start of something new.

## Taking advantage of perspective

The GoPro sees the world through an ultra-wide-angle view, as shown in Figure 6-11, so you don't have the luxury of varying focal length to alter subject size when you're shooting from a fixed distance. Instead of treating this limitation as a liability, let it work to your advantage by concentrating on the way you frame the subject matter.

The first time someone loaned me a fish-eye lens for my SLR (single lens reflex camera), I was amazed by how much of the world it captured. At one point, I placed the camera on the curb to get a low-angle view of Times

Square, and a cab blocked my shot as I pressed the shutter. After the film was processed, I saw an amazingly distorted image of the taxi, even though it couldn't have been more than two feet from the camera. The GoPro provides a similar experience, and because you're not always nearby, it may deliver similar surprises.

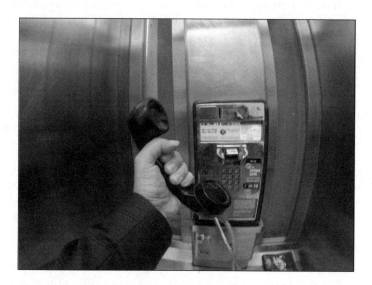

Figure 6-11: Ultra-wide-angle view.

# Thinking About Where to Put Your GoPro

Most cameras can only be mounted on a tripod or handheld. The GoPro, however, can go anywhere. This section focuses on ways to maximize your opportunities when out shooting with the camera.

## Grabbing static shots

By its very nature, the GoPro thrives on action conditions, but that doesn't mean you're not going to need a static shot every now and again. A *static shot* is a still shot of a scene with very little or no activity. Think of it as being the movie version of a photograph. The length of the shot depends on the context.

Here are a few reasons to use a static shot:

- ✔ **Setting a scene:** A wide shot of a stadium before the big game, a downtown block on a Sunday morning, or a local landmark on a fall day can open the film to provide a sense of place.

- **Depicting a living creature that isn't moving:** Static shots don't always involve inanimate objects. You might take a static shot of your dog taking a nap, an athlete meditating before an event, or your dad snoozing on the couch.

- **Focusing on details:** Depending on what you're shooting in the movie, concentrating on a key part of the scene gives the viewer a sense of the subject. For example, you can mount the camera on your motocross bike for an action movie.

## Using motion

The GoPro allows you to use motion as a creative device. Besides capturing an action sequence with incredible sharpness and exposure, you can alter the speed of the action, creating both slow motion and accelerated activity onscreen. Here are some ways to alter the normal rate of motion:

- **Slow motion:** The GoPro offers a variety of frame rates with most resolution settings. Frame rates differ from model to model, with the Hero4 Black Edition offering the most options. If you want to shoot slow motion, you should pick the highest frame-rate setting available — generally, 120 frames per second (fps) or higher. Then you need to process the footage (more on that in Chapter 11).

- **Fast motion:** Although you can achieve this effect by playing with the frame rate in GoPro Studio Edit, you can also shoot a time-lapse movie. The latter technique surely provides better quality because the footage is constructed of individual still images.

## Finding your unique point of view

Having a camera that provides a unique view of the world can stimulate your creative approach to arranging a scene. That's why it's important to find the best position for your GoPro by changing its position — higher, lower, or even tilted — to make a shot more interesting.

Where you position the camera speaks loudly about the message you're trying to convey and affects how you edit your movie.

Try including some of these shots in your next movie:

- **High angle:** Whether you mount your GoPro on a pole or use some kind of handheld extension device, you elevate the camera and change the perspective, providing a more graphical composition of the frame. Besides providing a unique perspective, this shot can make the audience look down on the character, perhaps to depict weakness. It can also produce a bobblehead effect when you're shooting a person (see Figure 6-12).

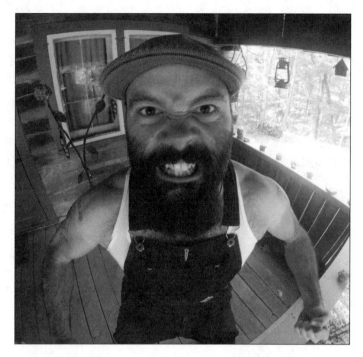

©The Rev J. Peyton/bigdamnband.com

**Figure 6-12:** Bobblehead effect.

- **Bird's-eye:** Although this shot isn't easy for most cameras, GoPro makes it possible to capture an angle that would make Alfred Hitchcock proud. Positioning the camera high and directly above the action creates a topographical view, often making common objects unrecognizable.

- **Low angle:** Mounting the camera as low as possible and pointing it upward provides another dynamic option for your movie. With this perspective, you can change the horizon. A low-angle shot also shows the viewer something he or she normally doesn't see. You can also use it to show the perspective of a child.

- **Dutch angle:** Intentionally tilting the frame provides a refreshing break in conventional viewing. This perspective, which is popular in horror flicks, independent films, and music videos, can depict alienation, uncertainty, and tension. Whenever possible, try to use this creative device; it can make your movies more visually appealing. But use it sparingly. It gets old rather quickly.

### Moving the camera

Because your GoPro is mostly attached to a mount, it's going to move with the subject. At other times, you can also use it like a conventional movie camera when it comes to following the action or making a visual statement. Consider the following:

- **Pan:** A sweeping motion of the scene that goes side to side.
- **Tilt:** It's the camera's version of looking up, down, or up and down.
- **Tracking shot:** A means of using the focal length to draw the subjects closer or further away while shooting the scene.

## Working with the GoPro App

The GoPro App lets you control the camera and see what's going on. All the tips in this chapter about managing the contents of the frame won't matter much unless you can see exactly what you're doing. Also, because the GoPro isn't always in front of you, using your smartphone with the GoPro App is the only game in town.

### Controlling the camera remotely

Because of the interesting places you can put a GoPro, you're rarely close to the camera. That's what makes the GoPro App so invaluable. You can not only see the shot, but also have complete access to camera controls. Among other things, you can start and stop the recording, adjust camera functions, switch modes, and check your battery level from a distance.

### Monitoring the shoot

The first time I picked up a GoPro, it felt like something was missing. Of course, that something was the viewfinder. Most GoPro cameras do not have a viewfinder, nor do they need one since the camera is often in the middle of action that you are not. That's what makes the GoPro App, as seen in Figure 6-13, so important: It allows you to monitor the scene from a safe distance and make mode and settings changes.

### Viewing footage on a tablet or smartphone

After you shoot your footage, you can watch it on a mobile device. In film lingo, this footage represents dailies you can watch anywhere you want. You can even browse and delete content from your camera to free space or include more compelling footage.

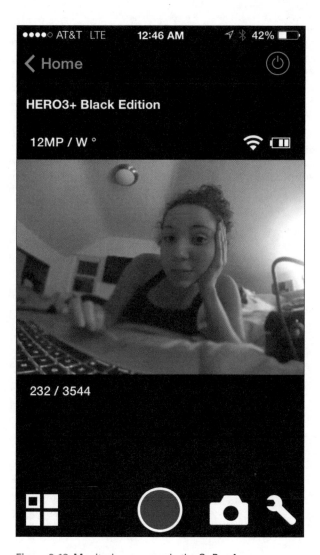

**Figure 6-13:** Monitoring a scene in the GoPro App.

# *Shooting Some Variations*

Editing a movie is a lot like assembling a jigsaw puzzle: Success depends on putting the right pieces together. Puzzle pieces are predetermined, but your movie isn't. That's why you need to capture variations in your setup shots and cutaways.

Don't be stingy when it comes to shooting your movie. That extra footage can not only better capture your movie, but also add more flexibility when it comes time for editing. So why settle for a single take when you can capture it several more times to get it perfect? Besides, it wasn't unusual for a movie to have a 20:1 ratio when it was shot on film. You're shooting on a card that you can download and erase.

But making sure you've shot enough variations of each scene differs from haphazardly capturing whatever you see and expecting to turn it into a cohesive movie. Instead, carefully decide the content of your film and then make sure that the technical and aesthetic settings match your intentions.

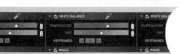  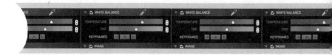

# 7

# Mastering the Light

## In This Chapter

▶ Seeing what makes up light

▶ Knowing the secrets of light sources

▶ Managing white balance

▶ Making the most of light

*L*ight defines how we record the world and communicate ideas through movies. But not just any light will do, so don't expect it to transform your GoPro movie into anything spectacular unless it's appropriate for the scene. Have you ever been in an old house that uses dingy fluorescent tubes for bathroom illumination? If so, you know that the light makes you look like an alien — not just any alien, but a sick one. Compare that with your appearance in a mirror adorned with an array of soft tungsten bulbs. Now, that's better.

It's important to think of light much in the same way that a painter thinks of paint. She doesn't throw it on haphazardly (unless her name is Jackson Pollock). Instead, she applies the paint very deliberately, creating both form and detail. Great lighting shares this idea and provides an intoxicating mystique to a scene.

Understanding the intricacies and physics of light can help you master it. This chapter is all about light.

## Seeing the Color and Temperature of Light

Ever wonder why the picture of your cat on the living-room couch had a yellow cast or what caused Uncle Freddie to look so blue that he looked like he needed some resuscitation? Funny things can happen when the color isn't quite right. Sometimes, we can live with it; at other times, it's a challenge. Though many scenes captured on a GoPro thrive on excitement, the color should nonetheless appear natural.

The good news: Odd color isn't a flaw in the camera. The bad news: The camera wasn't set properly to capture the color temperature of the light source or the automatic white balance was fooled.

## Taking color temperature

Our brains can differentiate color, but we may not notice when a shadow looks a little blue or when there's a limited spectrum of color in the mall parking lot (see Figure 7-1). When you capture a scene with a camera, however, colors become quite apparent, because different light sources have their own ways of producing color.

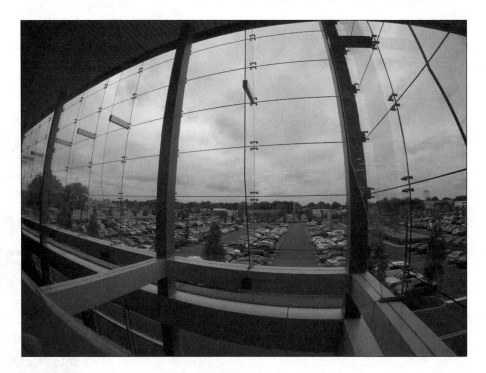

Figure 7-1: Overcast rendering of the mall parking lot.

If you view a piece of white paper under lights ranging from an indoor light bulb to the midday sun, you'd still see it as white. That's simply a function of your visual memory. The camera will record it as white, too, but it may render it with a blue or orange tinge, because the color temperature may differ from what the camera is set to record.

Celsius and Fahrenheit temperatures help you determine what to wear when you leave the house; Kelvin temperatures (K), however, measure light. Kelvin color temperatures range from candlelight at 1800 K to overcast sky at 11000 K.

Table 7-1 lists color temperatures in Kelvins for a few common light sources.

| Table 7-1 | Color Temperatures |
|---|---|
| *Light Source* | *Temperature in Kelvins (K)* |
| Candlelight | 1800 K |
| Rising or setting sun | 2200–2800 K |
| Incandescent household bulb | 2800 K |
| Tungsten light | 3200 K |
| Daylight | 5500 K |
| Sun on overcast day | 6000–8000 K |
| Shade | 7000 K |
| Cloudy day | 8000–10,000 K |

### Understanding white balance

*White balance* refers to setting the camera to record light at its proper color temperature. Simply put, a camera renders a white piece of paper as white when its white balance is set properly for a specific type of light. Many cameras, including the GoPro, adjust to the proper setting automatically, but automatic settings are often fooled.

One way to counteract disparity in color is to set white balance on the camera to match a specific situation. I cover this topic in more detail in "Setting White Balance" later in this chapter.

## Comparing Light Sources

We humans see light as the antidote to darkness, but we're often oblivious to its physical properties, such as direction, harshness, and color temperature. Our visual memory kicks in, and the only criterion is seeing what we need to see.

A camera, however, has no visual memory. Instead, it relies on its settings. Like Mr. Spock from *Star Trek*, it deals with color and exposure in a logical way. But even when you set the GoPro on automatic and let it adjust to each circumstance, success isn't guaranteed. Sometimes, a scene reproduces with a color cast, which may not match other scenes. You may have a bluish tint on one shot and a cyan cast on another.

Although the GoPro has a fairly intuitive automatic white balance (see "Setting White Balance" later in this chapter), an important part of mastering GoPro moviemaking is understanding the behaviors of different kinds of light.

## Sunlight

The primary source of light on the planet resides an average distance of 93 million miles away. The sun provides summer pleasure, vitamin D, and sometimes electrical power, and it's also the recorded image's best friend.

When you're making movies outdoors, the quality of sunlight changes continuously throughout the day with regard to both intensity and color. If you were to start shooting at daybreak, for example, you'd reap the benefits of soft morning light. Dawn light is much warmer than the daylight setting on your GoPro (5500 K; see "Taking color temperature," earlier in this chapter), so it reproduces as an orange glow on the subject. It's also coming from just above the horizon, so it's not lighting the subject from overhead.

Even though light still flatters the subject a couple of hours into the morning, the quality of light begins to transform as the sun gets higher. High noon puts the sun directly overhead, producing far less warmth and harsher illumination.

Some days, the clouds roll in, making the afternoon overcast. That type of light isn't great for the beach but not too bad for shooting a movie, thanks to the nicely diffused illumination. It lacks the warmth of early morning light, but you could tweak it in postproduction.

Later in the day, when the sun breaks through the clouds, the color balance of the scene takes on the warmth of early morning, but in the reverse direction (see Figure 7-2).

Clearly, shooting outdoors covers a wide range of color temperatures. It's vital that you make manual adjustments when necessary, as I discuss in "Bathing in sunlight" later in this chapter.

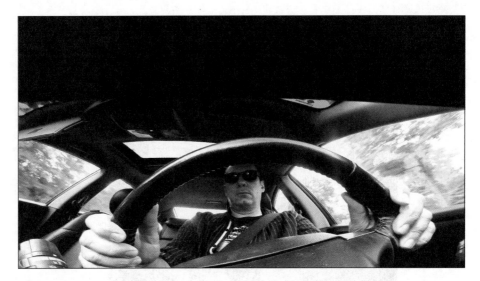

Figure 7-2: Beautiful light from late-afternoon sun.

## Household lights

When it comes to indoor moviemaking, most of the time you're going to shoot under household lighting conditions. But the game has changed with the incandescent light bulb we all knew, loved, and occasionally burned our fingers on being phased out. In its place, more economical light forms are taking over. Some share similarities with formerly bulbous light sources, while others have their own qualities.

### CFL bulbs

Until very recently, most lamps used incandescent bulbs (discussed later in this chapter), but these days, you're more likely to see compact fluorescent light (CFL) bulbs (see Figure 7-3).

CFLs are so common now that you can find them almost everywhere, but they have many variations, which makes it hard to nail down the exact behavior of each one. Because they produce light differently from incandescent bulbs, they're not very predictable when it comes to shooting your movie. Instead of heating a filament to burn brightly, they produce light through a jolt of electricity that excites vapor in the tube, sharing behavior with their taller cousin, the fluorescent tube.

But ingenuity is a wonderful thing. Because these lights are so popular and cheap to operate, they've been engineered to create various light settings, including a full spectrum of color. That makes them great for lighting television and movie sets.

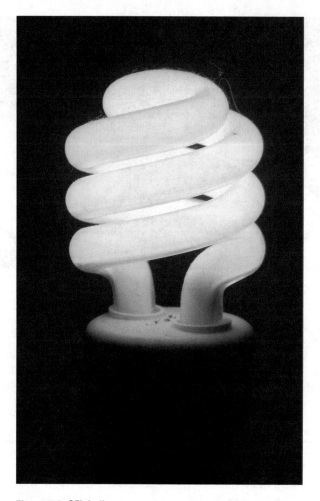

Figure 7-3: CFL bulb.

### *LED bulbs*

Watches, scoreboards, and television use it, and now so does the lighting in your home. The LED lamp is quickly becoming one of the most efficient forms of artificial light on the planet. Consisting of an array of light emitting diodes, they collectively form illumination in places where bulbs used to reside.

An interesting quality about some of these light forms is that the same bulb can create any color you like, and can be controlled from your smartphone or device. They screw into lamps and fixtures, and can be combined to make any combinations of colors you choose.

On the bright side (pun intended), LED lighting offers the most control over the light. Conversely, it is expensive and does not provide a high light output.

### Halogen bulbs

A true incandescent light source, these lamps offer a high output and naturally produce a full spectrum of color that generally matches tungsten.

Halogen bulbs are found in many places, including automotive headlamps, projector bulbs, and studio lighting. While they usually don't resemble a traditional household bulb, some types now include a screw base for use in lamp and fixture sockets.

These lamps have a wide variety of uses and come in various sizes and types. On the downside, they get very hot and are sometimes used for heating purposes. Ever hear of a halogen oven?

### Incandescent bulbs

Incandescent light bulbs are traditional light bulbs, the ones that appear above cartoon characters' heads whenever they have a great idea. Brightness varies from 25-watt appliance bulbs to the 60-, 75-, and 100-watt bulbs used in reading lamps. Flood lighting can go to 150 watts, but generally anything equivalent to 65 watts is more common.

Currently, incandescent bulbs are being phased out, but people have stocked up on them. So they are still being widely used, and you may find yourself shooting under incandescent light.

## Fluorescent lights

Tubes of light seem like perfect ways to deliver illumination. These long, bright sticks are efficient, effective, and used everywhere from basements and garages to factories and offices. They make light through a jolt of electricity exciting vapor in the tube. While generally not ideal for shooting a movie, there are numerous types engineered to produce a full spectrum of color. Some are even used for television and movie lighting. Here's what you need to know:

- **Daylight-balanced tubes:** While comparatively lower in output than an incandescent bulb, they offer mass illumination. Sometimes four separate tubes can produce the same output, albeit by using a wider, more collective approach.

- **Mixed lighting makes a good picture:** Look at any office building and notice the variations in color cast. Lighting your movie with tungsten and allowing the variations of fluorescent light in the background produces a complementary cast that works to your advantage.

- **Not a harsh bone in its, err, the subject's body:** Because illumination comes from a wide bank of soft lamps, it produces a nice soft illumination. As a result, it hides minor blemishes, making many actors fans of it.

✔ **No heat buildup:** There's a reason these are also known as "cool lights." Trust me, they're a welcome alternative, especially when using a multiple light tungsten setup in the studio or location area. Fluorescent illumination doesn't create excess heat, and you can touch the bulbs.

## Candlelight

If the sun is the Big Kahuna, candlelight is the little guy. It's the warmest and least powerful light source (below 2000 K; refer to "Taking color temperature," earlier in this chapter) range, and by itself, it can barely cover a foot. But candlelight is still light. A group of candles can illuminate a whole scene, lending it a warm and cozy feeling. Because the GoPro gets very close, it can work nicely for candlelit scenes.

## Neon lights

Iconic neon signs such as "Bar" are glass sculptures with illuminated colored light running through their tubes. Neon is reminiscent of the night, and it looks cool, as shown in Figure 7-4.

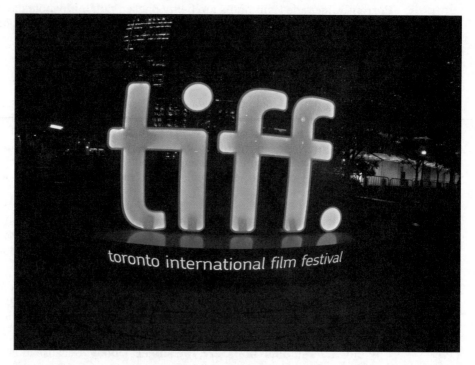

**Figure 7-4:** CFL bulbs inside bring the translucent red sign to life.

## Outdoor lights (HID)

Lighting up the night takes a lot of power, and that can get expensive for whoever pays the bill. So the goal in illuminating massive spaces is producing the most light for the least money. Many government agencies and businesses use a special kind of outdoor illumination: high-intensity discharge (HID) lights.

Like CFLs (see "CFL bulbs," earlier in this chapter), HID lights excite a gas inside a glass tube, producing cheap, bright light. They come in three varieties:

✓ **Sodium vapor:** What you regard as a streetlight, lighting experts and city designers know as a sodium-vapor lamp on a pole. Look closely, and you'll notice that its light has a yellowish cast (see Figure 7-5).

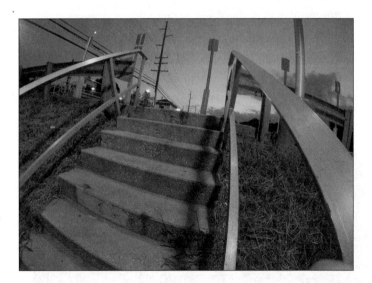

Figure 7-5: Sodium-vapor street light.

✓ **Mercury vapor:** Mercury-vapor lamps are far less flattering to most subjects than sodium-vapor lamps are, because they produce greenish illumination from exciting mercury gas. This color makes them problematic when it comes to video. When it comes to producing the most economical illumination, these guys are great for parking lots, garages, and even some school gymnasiums. On average, they have a color temperature of about 4200 K (see "Taking color temperature," earlier in this chapter).

✔ **Metal halide:** Like the other HID lamps, metal-halide lamps produce light by exciting weird gases, but unlike those lamps, they also produce a full spectrum of color. The reason for their hybrid nature? Metal-halide lamps are used to light many outdoor stadiums, and nobody wants to see anything but the richest, most saturated color when watching football on a bigscreen TV.

## Setting White Balance (Black Edition)

If you're feeling adventurous or simply want to control the color temperature of a scene on your GoPro, feel free to change the White Balance setting. By default, your GoPro is set to Auto, but you have other options, including these:

✔ **Auto:** Adjusts automatically to the color temperature of the light source.

✔ **3000K:** Works well for capturing indoor scenes.

✔ **5500K:** Lets you manually balance color outdoors.

✔ **6500K:** Matches the color temperature of moderately overcast skies and some forms of fluorescent lighting.

✔ **Camera RAW:** Records a RAW file so you can adjust the color temperature during the postproduction process (see Figure 7-6).

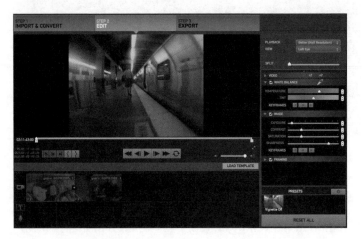

Figure 7-6: Color correction in GoPro Studio Edit.

Here's how you can change the White Balance setting:

1. **Press the Power/Mode button to scroll through the menus until you get to the Settings menu.**

The Settings menu's icon looks like a wrench.

2. **Press the Shutter/Select button to select Settings.**

3. **Make sure Protune is on.**

Otherwise the White Balance menu will not be visible.

4. **Scroll until you get to capture settings.**

Enter it by pressing the Shutter/Select button.

5. **Go to the White Balance option.**

6. **Use the Shutter/Select to select one of the following options: Auto, 3000K, 5500K, 6500K, or Camera Raw, and press the Power/Mode button to set it.**

# Working with the Light You Have

Because many action sequences take place outdoors, you need the sun for illumination. That big, flaming ball of fire in the sky offers bright, diverse, and complimentary illumination. It not only flatters the subject, but it's also free. But that doesn't mean there isn't a slight price to pay. It's a passive light form that leaves you with no control over it, and you just have to accept its direction of light, the shadow it creates, or its light quality. Seems like a fair price to pay when you consider what you get in return.

One day, the light renders warmly against a rich blue sky, and the next day it's completely different. Sometimes the background sky renders palely; other times it's completely overcast. The sun is always in the sky, but that stuff in between — you know the clouds and haze — can affect what the sun can do on a predictable basis.

Consider the following:

- **Watch out for lens flare:** Because the GoPro is so wide, there's a greater possibility for lens flare. That means you need to be careful.

- **Try to use sunlight from a lower angle:** This creates the most flattering illumination, and it's generally warmer too.

- **Avoid overhead light:** When the sun is beating straight down on the subject, it's not flattering and creates harsh shadows.

- **Take advantage of an overcast day:** Direct sunlight is sometimes harsh on the subject because it skims across the face and creates shadow and texture. Most people don't like it. Clouds come between the sun and the subject and act as a diffuser, presenting the subject in a more flattering illumination. Just watch out for white patches of sky.

## *Bathing in sunlight*

Here are a few ways to make the most of sunlight:

- **Work the angles.** I don't mean working the angles in a grifter sort of way; rather, I mean catching sunlight from different angles.

- **Shoot early or late.** Sunlight becomes more intense as the sun rises higher in the sky, and color temperature increases as the day goes on. A sunny-day color temperature is about 5500K (see "Taking color temperature," earlier in this chapter) when the sun reaches its highest point. The temperature gets warmer as dusk approaches.

  Whenever possible, it's best to shoot your movie early in the morning or late in the afternoon. At those times, the sun is at an angle that produces the most flattering illumination and the warmest tone (refer to Figure 7-2).

- **Take advantage of clouds.** Although it can be beautiful, direct sunlight can also produce harsh illumination. Most people don't like being photographed in full sunlight. But cloud cover between the sun and the subject works like a giant diffuser, bathing subjects in more-flattering light.

- **Avoid shooting at noon.** *High Noon* is a great title for a movie but not a great time to shoot it. When the sun is beating straight down on the subject, it's not flattering and creates harsh shadows.

## *Managing artificial illumination*

When the sun decides to call it a day, the nightscape comes to life, and individual forms of artificial lighting don't play by the same set of rules as the sun. There are many types of artificial light, each with its own behavior (see "Comparing Light Sources," earlier in this chapter). Here are a few potential problems of shooting under artificial light:

- **Annoying color casts:** Not all light sources produce a full spectrum of color, especially HID lamps (see "Outdoor lights [HID]," earlier in this chapter), which you're likely to find on a city street or country road. Depending on the way the light source produces light, the scene can render with a yellowish or cyan tinge.

  The good news is that a meticulous white-balance setting can eliminate a color cast; the bad news is that it may deplete the scene of all color. HID lights produce a single color, so when you correct the bad color, no others are left.

- **Unpredictable results:** Sometimes, you don't notice the effect of color or contrast on your smartphone's screen until it's too late.

✔ **Harsh shadows:** Contrasty, splotchy light creates shadows that can wreak havoc. When you adjust for these shadows, the highlights may blown out. Fix the highlights, and the middle tones become shadowy.

In the following sections, I show you how to solve problems with several types of light sources.

### Working with incandescent bulbs

It's possible to use an array of incandescent bulbs to light your movie, but their effectiveness depends on a variety of factors, including wattage, placement, and positioning. Some tips on working with incandescent bulbs follow.

✔ **Move it from the subject.** It's hard to get more basic than simply moving the light away, especially if it's a lamp.

✔ **Reduce its brightness.** If it has a dimmer, turn it down. Other options include using a neutral density gel filter over your GoPro or trying a lower-wattage bulb.

✔ **Remember that fall-off happens quickly:** When the subject is relatively close (but not too close) to the light source, you can capture adequate exposure. But the range of light doesn't go very far.

✔ **Watch for hot spots.** Because the camera covers such a wide angle, it's nearly impossible to keep the actual light out of the frame. Monitor it from the GoPro App to compose the scene so the light is either out of the picture or doesn't ruin the scene.

### Coping with CFLs

Here's what you need to know about which CFLs can work to your advantage and which ones to avoid:

✔ **Hot it's not:** Fluorescent illumination is considered a cool light form because it doesn't create excess heat. Not only does this means you can touch the bulbs (if you were so inclined), but also because they keep the room from getting unbearably hot. That makes illumination the subject from a nearby CFL far more bearable.

✔ **Be careful of the color:** While many CFL bulbs provide the characteristics of a traditional household bulb, some behave more like economical fluorescent tubes. That means a dim greenish cast that looks terrible when recorded. Use your eyes to help judge the quality of light.

✔ **Hot spots need not apply:** While lighting found around the home is not incredibly bright, it can still produce spectral hot spots (bright light reflections) either because the light source is in the scene, reflecting on a bright surface, or flaring into the lens. It's imperative to use your smartphone to monitor the scene when using GoPro indoors.

### Making the best of fluorescence

Old school fluorescents produce a sickly green light, but when combined on the scene with light sources of other color temperature, it suddenly becomes just another part of the scene. Look at any office building and notice the variations in color cast. Consider the following:

- **Try to work with daylight-balanced:** While far less bright that an incandescent light bulb, illumination from a mass array of fluorescent tubes produces adequate lighting by using a wider, more collective approach.

- **Take advantage of mixed light:** Lighting your movie with tungsten and allowing the variations of fluorescent light in the background produces a complementary cast that works to your advantage.

- **Take a white balance:** Or at least see how your GoPro treats it on the automatic setting. Fluorescent lighting differs with color output; even when the lighting looks good to the eye, it may not reproduce as naturally as you may like.

### Capturing candlelight

Take the following pointers into consideration when you work with candlelight:

- **Be careful.** It's worth repeating that a candle is a fire, and fire can burn.

- **The subject is light.** A candle is one of the few light sources that you can keep in a scene without hoping that people think you're just being "ironic." Candles make great props as well as lighting the scene. For a table scene, measure the exposure from the candle, and don't worry too much if the subject is a bit underexposed.

- **There's strength in numbers.** A single candle usually isn't enough to light a scene, but a group of them becomes a force to reckon with. Use a candelabra or multiple candle holders to create soft, warm illumination.

### Loving the way that neon glows

Here are a few ways to work with neon:

- **Use a wide range of exposures.** Neon light is quite flexible when it comes to exposure. Underexpose it to get rich, saturated color. Overexpose it to open the ambient portions of the scene without losing much color from the lamp.

- **Establish the location.** Think about neon as a scene-setter. Just about any neon light can establish a scene, including a sign for a restaurant, hotel, or bowling alley.

- **Take advantage of reflections.** These colorful lights aren't overly bright, but they reflect their rich colors on nearby surfaces. The effect is exponentially powerful when a neon sign is reflected on a rainy sidewalk.

### Handling HID lights

HID light is great for finding your car keys in a parking lot or looking at city landmarks at night, but it's terrible for making movies.

Now, I said *terrible,* not *impossible,* because there are ways to take advantage of HIDs. Here are some ways to make this type of light work for you:

- **A little goes a long way.** Instead of trying to fully correct the color, just reduce it slightly. You're still have a color cast, but it won't be overwhelming anymore. The footage can pass for a street scene, especially when you have supplemental light coming from stores, neon signs, or the taillights of passing cars.

- **Shoot at twilight.** Twilight still has ambient light and a purplish sky that looks great when you position your subject against it.

- Because a sodium-vapor lamp's illumination is created by excited gas, there's nothing left to do after you correct the color. So if you take a white balance of the scene, use a blue filter to neutralize the yellow cast, or attempt to correct it in postproduction, all that would remain is a monochromatic rendering of the subject. Unlike an incandescent light source that can be color corrected thanks to its full spectrum of color, these light forms only produce a single color. It you had to place a color temperature on this type of lamp, it would be comparable to tungsten, making it around 3000K.

It's a good idea to take a white balance under metal-halide light. Depending on the specific type of lamp, color temperature can range from 3000K to 6000K or higher (see "Taking color temperature," earlier in this chapter). Check and reset the white balance often.

## Creating Your Own Light

Because natural light (the sun) isn't always around, and artificial light leaves you in a passive role, bring your own light to the scene. The pros have done that since the early days, because using their own lights allows them to actively control light direction, intensity, and color temperature. Now you can do the same.

Lighting a scene can be as simple as using a single bulb and reflector or as elaborate as employing a light kit with soft boxes, umbrellas, stands, and booms. As long as you have some way of lighting the scene and can keep the lights out of view from your GoPro, feel free to light it up.

## Basic lighting

Lighting a scene means using the right materials in the right way. The way you light your scene can help establish what you're trying to say without the audience's noticing a thing. Viewers absorb the movie as a whole, with lighting, action, and sound quality working together to sustain their attention.

Here are the basic lights you might use:

- **Main light:** As the name implies, the *main light* is the key source of light in a scene. Whether that light is the sun, an outdoor lamp, or your light kit, its main job is to illuminate the subject. If you place the main light at a 45-degree angle from the subject, half of the subject renders in shadow, which can be quite dramatic.

- **Fill light:** The *fill light* illuminates the subject from the side not affected by the main light. Depending on the subject, you can position the fill light at a higher or lower angle than the subject to fill in the shadow areas. The fill light can also be a reflector that redirects illumination from the main light. When you're shooting outdoors, the fill light may be a large white reflector bouncing sunlight back on the subject.

  Just make sure that the fill light doesn't overpower the main light.

- **Back light (or hair light):** With the front of the subject adequately covered, you use *back light* to add depth to the scene and separate the subject from the background. Position this light high and off to the side, at a 45-degree angle from the subject.

## Tungsten lighting

Tungsten lights are used for professional lighting in the studio and on location. This type of bulb produces light by heating the tungsten filament inside until it glows (see Figure 7-7). Studio tungsten bulbs can go as high as 1,000 watts and generally produce a color temperature of 3200 K (see "Taking color temperature," earlier in this chapter).

Tungsten lighting comes in many forms, including the icon giant lights used on movie set. Some tungsten lights use a glass lens called a Fresnel (developed for use in lighthouses) that maximizes the light's potential. Studio lighting uses a combination of Fresnel lenses and reflectors to concentrate light on the subject. These lights produce a full spectrum of color like the sun and can be moved wherever they're needed.

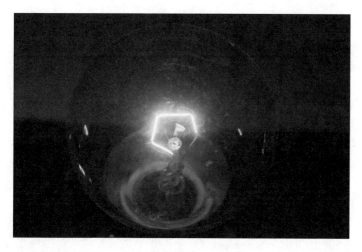

Figure 7-7: Heated tungsten filament creates light.

## Nonconventional lighting

Conforming to conventional lighting is considered to be a fundamental concept of moviemaking. But what about using nonconventional lighting? You can improvise with just about anything that emits light, such as the following:

- **Work lights:** You may have seen work-light kits at home-improvement superstores. The lights use some form of tungsten bulbs; many kits have stands and reflectors. The light is harsh but easy to smooth out by finding a creative way to diffuse it. The kits are cheap — a bonus if you're on a limited budget.

- **Flashlight or lantern:** These light sources aren't as unbelievable or impractical as you may think. They're self-contained, low-intensity light kits that you can use in a jam or for some creative effect.

- **Television screen:** If the subject is close to a television set and the GoPro is close to both, it's hard to imagine a softer, more interesting light source than the TV screen. Just tune the set to a nonbroadcast channel and position the subject close to the screen.

- **Glow sticks:** They're not bright enough for illuminating a scene, but they often work in situations in which the subject is light. Not only do they provide illumination, but their intense, saturated color makes for a great subject too.

## Taming tungsten bulbs

If a tungsten light source is too harsh for your GoPro movie, consider the following options:

✔ **Move it away from the subject.** It's hard to get more basic than simply moving the light away.

✔ **Reduce its brightness.** If the light has a dimmer, turn it down, or use a lower-wattage lamp.

✔ **Soften the light.** Put the light in a soft box to get close so you can bathe the subject in bright but flattering light.

✔ **Reflect the light.** You can turn the light around and bounce it into a reflective umbrella. If you're in a jam with the budget or don't have an umbrella, use a piece of diffusion material over the light source instead.

✔ **Focus the light.** Narrow down how much of the light illuminates the subject.

✔ **Use a filter.** Use a neutral-density gel filter to cut down a couple of stops of light.

# Using Light Effectively

Like many things in life, shooting under the right lighting conditions depends on the time of day, your ability to think on your feet, and recognizing the opportunity. It's important to understand how light behaves so you're ready to effectively capture the subject. Here's how to use light effectively.

## Wait for the right light

The sun flatters subjects early in the morning and early in the evening; in the middle of the day, it's not as effective. Twilight is the narrow span of time between sundown and dusk; the sun is below the horizon but still emits some light. This time of night is a sweet spot, thanks to its rich blue or purple background (see Figure 7-8). But twilight lasts only 20 minutes or so, so you have to act fast.

If you have time, wait for the right light. You have only a short window of time to make the shot work.

## Work with the light you have

Color casts aren't intrinsically bad, and sometimes, they have a place. The normally unflattering cast of a mercury-vapor lamp can emulate an otherworldly experience, for example, just as a street scene lit with sodium-vapor can lend warmth to a subject. (I cover both types of lighting in "Outdoor lights [HID]," earlier in this chapter.)

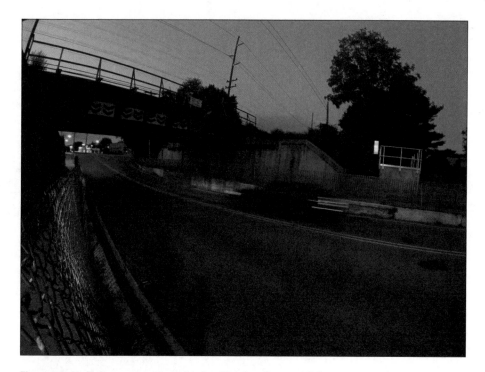

**Figure 7-8:** Twilight scene with a mix of artificial and natural light.

When the sun goes down, artificial light dominates the scene. Sometimes it does so in an unflattering way, with each light source producing a dominant color of illumination. Separately, this artificial light is problematic because it produces a single color cast. But when you combine artificial light sources, they collectively show various colors. Put artificial light against a twilight sky, and you have something unique and often beautiful.

## Use colored gels

Gels work wonders when you want to adjust the color of a scene, do something creative, or make a statement. You can use a colored gel over a light to spice up the background.

## Avoid light pollution

Pollution doesn't apply just to dirty beaches and belching factory pipes; it also refers to the interplay among lights in a scene. One light can spill to the coverage area of the next, producing hot spots, color variations, and odd shadows. In addition, it's likely to create lens flare (see the nearby sidebar) because the GoPro captures such a wide view.

## Lens-flare alert

Although it's common for light from an unintended light source to shine into your lens, it's even more common with the GoPro, due to its wide lens. Lens flare occurs when the axis of the lens gets too close to a light source. Sometimes, lens flare acts as an artistic device; more often, it makes you look like you're not observant enough.

Here are a few ways to deal with lens flare:

- **Remain alert.** Look at the light in the scene from the camera's perspective, and double-check it in the GoPro App on your smartphone.

- **Adjust the camera's position.** Because you can't use a lens hood or matte box with a GoPro (its angle of view is too wide), if you can't move the light, your only option is to reposition the camera.

- **Accept it.** Sometimes, you have no choice but to accept lens flare. It might even complement your movie. When you're shooting a street scene at night, for example, flare from the lights of passing cars seems natural.

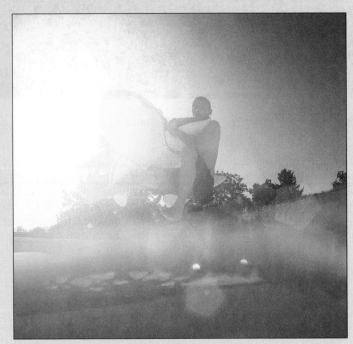

©istockphoto.com/piola666 Image #36308186

In a perfect world, having the light at your back is the ideal way to use a GoPro, but it's not always possible to do so. That's why it's important to strategically place your camera and monitor the scene before recording to prevent light pollution.

## Light the scene efficiently

Sometimes, a portion of the light source doesn't reach the subject, either because it strays out of the way due to improper bouncing or isn't bright enough. Make sure that the light is properly directed to the subject and close enough to be effective.

## Deal with problematic ambient light

Whether it's a window leaking bright light or a glaring streetlamp, stray light can ruin your shot. Combat it by repositioning the camera or blocking the offending light with a card, sheet, or anything else that prevents it from reaching your subject.

# 8

# Of Sound Movie and Body

## In This Chapter

▶ Breaking down microphone types

▶ Avoiding audio pitfalls

▶ Monitoring your audio

*I*f you showed a group of viewers two movie clips — one a high-definition (HD) video with slightly distorted audio quality and the other a standard-definition (SD) video with clear sound — and asked them which video is better quality, chances are that they'd pick the SD version. That's because the better your movie sounds, the more an audience will appreciate it.

Sound completes the sensory experience of a film, so always make sure that your movies sound great. That's easier said than done with the GoPro, though, because it doesn't always capture sound effectively. Maybe you didn't place it in the right location to capture the right sounds, or perhaps the limitations of the built-in microphone came back to haunt you. Lots of things can make audio capture on a GoPro less than perfect.

Although the GoPro can't handle every audio situation out of the box, a wide range of accessories can help you capture superior sound.

## Capturing Sound on the Scene

The GoPro allows you to use the same range of microphones as any other camcorder, though some mikes require an adapter that plugs into the camera or mixer and captures audio directly on the camera's memory card. DSLRs and some consumer-level camcorders generally use a 3.5mm (mini-plug), not much different from the one on your headphones, whereas more advanced models use the XLR input (that's the bigger one with the prongs). You can also record audio with an audio recorder, which bypasses the GoPro's memory card and captures sound as a separate file, which you can match with the video in your editing program (see Part III). If you have a professional-quality microphone that uses an XLR connection, you can use an adapter.

You will notice that your GoPro does not have a connection for either type of microphone. No need to worry. You can buy an inexpensive accessory (see Figure 8-1) that plugs into the mini USB connection on the camera. You can plug in a mini-plug microphone, as well as an adapter to use an XLR connection.

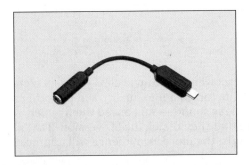

Figure 8-1: GoPro 3.5mm mic adapter lets you attach an external microphone to the camera.

All microphones and audio recorders have advantages and drawbacks, as you see in the following sections.

## Using a microphone

When you think of shooting a GoPro movie, capturing sound with a microphone is not the first thing that comes to mind. Most people start with the microphone that's built into the camera, but some move on to other microphone types when they need to capture sound in a special way.

### Capturing sound with the on-camera microphone

Whenever you record video on your GoPro, the camera captures both video and audio. That is, sound and picture come together in a single file on your memory card.

The GoPro's microphone (see Figure 8-2) provides acceptable results when conditions are perfect: The subject is near the camera and there's little, if any, ambient noise. Unfortunately, conditions are rarely perfect.

The GoPro's microphone

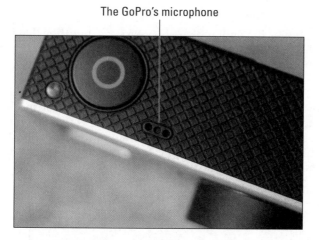

Figure 8-2: The GoPro's microphone.

On-camera microphones like the GoPro's have several drawbacks:

- They pick up all kinds of ambient sounds near the camera. Everything from barking dogs and screaming kids to planes passing overhead is recorded on your audio track.

- Even when those elements don't rear their ugly heads, the sound quality of the camera's microphone can lack depth and range, based on its proximity to the source.

- The GoPro is designed to capture unique visuals, not necessarily to record audio. Audio a secondary feature. When the best source of sound comes from the side of your GoPro, there's not much you can do about it.

On-camera microphones were never intended for serious recording. They were added as a cheap way to capture sound to go with video. Use the GoPro's mike to capture sound for reference, and use it when it's the only game in town.

### Adding a GoPro accessory microphone

All Hero2 and Hero3 GoPro cameras have a 3.5 mm mini-plug connector for internal audio, so theoretically, you can use any microphone that has a mini-plug. Microphones come in various types and price ranges, one of which may be perfect for your needs and budget.

### Using other microphone types

External microphones have their own sets of issues, but they definitely capture better audio than the GoPro's built-in mike. Here are several popular types of microphones:

✔ **Shotgun:** This long, narrow microphone (see Figure 8-3) picks up audio directly in front of it but not necessarily close to it. Basic models are attached to professional camcorders; dedicated versions are used in television studios and on boom poles at movie shoots and red-carpet events. Think of the shotgun mike as being the audio version of a telephoto lens.

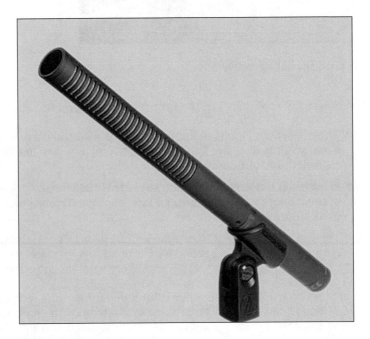

Figure 8-3: Shotgun microphone.

✔ **Directional:** The directional microphone is the most recognizable microphone on the planet. It's the type that singers use on stage, comedians use in clubs, and television news reporters hold in front of interview subjects, held close to the mouth to isolate ambient sound.

✔ **Lavalier:** Lavalier (or lapel) microphones (see Figure 8-4) are commonly used on television. The tiny device clips to the subject's clothing near his face and is wired either directly to the camera or to a transmitter on the subject. When used correctly, this microphone provides great audio and isn't visually obtrusive. When it's used improperly, the audio is a rustling, muffled mess.

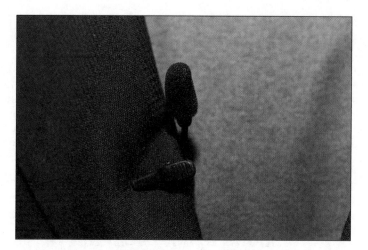

Figure 8-4: Lavalier microphone.

✔ **Camera-mounted:** Camera-mounted mikes are ideal for picking up natural sounds in the scene, such as the whoosh of a babbling brook or the pleasant sounds of a horse farm. They also work well for interviewing people when they're close enough to the camera — say, 4 to 7 feet away.

✔ **Stick:** Covers a wide range of microphone types that you hold with your hand in front of the subject, or in front of yourself. These mikes are usually tethered to the camera by an XLR cable, though some inexpensive models use a 3.5mm connection cable. It's ideal to use when interviewing a subject, or singing into the camera.

✔ **Boom:** Basically, it's a shotgun microphone connected to a pole so you can capture sound farther away from the camera.

✔ **Wireless:** Sometimes, you're just better off using a wireless microphone. Instead of tethering the camera to a cable, connect the microphone to a transmitter and a wireless receiver on the camera.

A wireless mike allows you to move independently of the camera as long as you're within range of its receiver. You don't have to worry about tripping over cables everywhere. Also, wireless requires less use of XLR cables, so the ones that you're using don't get stressed and stop working.

On the downside, wireless mikes have limited range — on average, 300 feet from the receiver, dead spots, interference, and noise can affect the recording. Also, if too many wireless microphones are using the same frequency, you may pick up a lot of noise, hum, and static.

## Capturing audio from distant subjects

If the subject is far from the camera, you can get the microphone closer by mounting it to a pole and holding it over the subject. Using a shotgun microphone tethered to the GoPro on a hand-held rack mount provides a definite improvement over your GoPro's built-in microphone. Just be careful to keep it out of the shot.

GoPro has a very wide view, so if the microphone encroaches on the frame, it's going to appear in the final shot. Another issue is that distant sounds don't record as cleanly as sounds closer to the microphone. The microphone's narrow band of capture limits some added noise, but unwanted sound can still be a problem.

## Mounting a mike on a GoPro

Unlike a traditional camcorder, the GoPro doesn't have an accessory mount that lets you attach an accessory microphone to the top of the camera, so you have to get creative. Here are some ideas:

- **Use a rack mount.** If you're going to hold your GoPro while recording sound, consider mounting the camera on a rack. It helps to use the tripod mount to do it because most racks depend on the tripod socket.

- **Mount the GoPro on yourself.** Use a headband or chest-harness mount for the camera, while you hold the microphone near the subject's face.

- **Tether the cable.** Mount the camera wherever you need it, and tether the microphone cable to the camera or portable audio recorder.

## Choosing the right mike for the job

Here are some common shooting situations and the right microphone to use in each situation:

- **Interviewing a moving subject: stick microphone.** The trick is to get the microphone close enough to a subject on the move without knocking out his teeth. Make sure that the microphone is no more than 9 inches from the subject.

    Be consistent about how far away you hold the mike. If you move closer or pull away, you can alter the audio level, which is similar to raising or lowering the volume — only worse. If you're not sure you can hold a constant position, have your sound person hold a boom microphone over the subject.

- **Capturing natural sound: on-camera microphone.** When you're recording natural sound with an on-camera microphone, it's important to get as close to the subject as possible. This can be a challenge when the audio source is at a different distance from the subject, so you may have to compromise between audio and video.

- ✓ **Shooting stationary talking subjects: lavalier microphone.** When you have a stationary subject, you can control the audio portion of your recording much better than you can in other situations. Because the subject isn't moving (or at least isn't going to move far), it's best to use a lavalier microphone to ensure that you capture sound at a consistent distance.

- ✓ **Shooting a movie scene: boom microphone.** If you're shooting a feature film, you're most likely capturing the audio on a separate recorder (see the next section), so camera-to-subject distance isn't an issue. The microphone and audio recorder can be much closer than the camera. The same can apply for your GoPro movie. Just make sure that the sound person holds the boom microphone appropriately. That means held from a consistent distance over the subject, and out of camera range.

## Using a digital audio recorder

Using a separate device to capture audio may seem to be complicated, but it's actually much simpler than you'd think. Also, it involves minimal risk with a great reward: optimal audio.

A digital audio recorder (see Figure 8-5) captures sound independently of the GoPro. Add the audio recording to the video in postproduction by matching it to the audio track captured by the camera, by using a plug-in for your editing software, or by using a separate sound application.

Here are some pointers for using a digital audio recorder:

- ✓ **Capture sound on the GoPro too.** It's essential to record a reference track to match the better-quality audio that the recorder captures. Later, you can discard the weaker track when editing in a more advanced program such as Final Cut Pro or Adobe Premiere.

- ✓ **Pick the proper audio format.** Digital audio recorders offer a wide range of audio format choices, but not all of them are right for movies. Choose a WAV or AIFF file. You can capture sound in MP3 format too, but the audio quality won't be very good.

- ✓ **Record on two or four channels.** A digital audio recorder lets you decide the number of channels you want to record and the audio format. Select four-channel recording if you want more control at various levels; then mix the sound down later.

- ✓ **Fine-tune your audio levels.** Make sure that audio levels are within range (that is, not peaking and creating distorted sound) by looking at the meters before you start recording. (For more information, see "Maintaining proper levels," later in this chapter.)

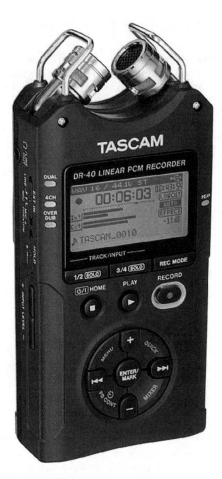

Figure 8-5: Digital audio recorder.

## Knowing audio formats

Here's a brief rundown of audio formats work that with Adobe Premiere Elements:

- **AIFF:** The Audio Interchange Format is an uncompressed audio file type developed by Apple. You can select a variety of bit rates. Regardless of which one you choose, it works in your timeline to match up with your movies.

- **MP3:** Although it's an option on audio recorders, it's not a good one for capturing sound for your movie. The MPEG-2 Audio Layer III encodes audio in a lossy format.

- **WAV:** What AIFF is to Apple, the Waveform (WAV) audio file format is to Windows. This common uncompressed audio format works on Macintosh and Windows computers and can be used in a variety of bit rates.

# Preventing Audio Problems

In capturing audio, some elements are clearly out of your power. What really matters is taking care of the ones that you can control. Sometimes, that's as simple as being aware of ambient noise on the scene. At other times, it means using a specific microphone technique.

## Working around background noise

The most common audio problems involve unwanted background noise. No matter where you are, something can ruin your audio capture. In urban areas, you may pick up honking horns, screeching truck brakes, or emergency-vehicle sirens. In the country, the problem may be tree branches rustling, crickets chirping, or animals making various sounds.

The microphone doesn't discriminate when it comes to sound, so it picks up what you want to record *and* an assortment of unwanted noises that can distract attention from the primary audio. It's your job to reduce as much background noise as possible.

To reduce background noise, try the following things:

- **Use your ears.** Your ears are made for more than just keeping your sunglasses from falling off your face. They're designed to pick up lots of different sounds. Before you press the Shutter/Select button to start recording, listen for any potential problems. If everything sounds good, Listen for noise patterns so you can shoot around traffic or wind gusts.
- **Stay away from noisy locations.** Airports, train stations, and high-traffic areas are obvious places to avoid, but chattering crowds and music blaring from passing cars also present challenges to recording audio. Whenever possible, position the microphone away from noisy locations.

## Maintaining proper levels

All but one GoPro lack a viewfinder, so maintaining audio levels isn't really possible because you can't see the meters. That's why it's important to use a separate audio recorder (see "Using a digital audio recorder," earlier in this chapter) when sound quality is high on your list. Watch its meters and use headphones to monitor the sound (see "Working with Other Sound Equipment," later in this chapter).

Audio should peak no higher than 12 decibels (dB). Otherwise, you'll get *clipping:* irreversible distortion caused by high audio levels. There's no sense in capturing audio if it's going to clip.

## Coping with wind

Using a separate microphone offers clear advantages over using the GoPro's on-camera microphone, but it may not be free of problems. Shooting on location puts you at the mercy of forces outside your control. Regardless of what kind of equipment you have or what you know about audio, the second you step outside a controlled environment, you're at the mercy of sound-related issues. Howling wind (or even just a whimpering one) can wreak havoc on a scene. Gusts can impede sound or render it unusable. Better-quality microphones reduce some wind-related problems, but only some.

The good news is that you can solve many sound-related dilemmas by using the proper techniques and accessories. Consider these coping strategies for shooting outdoors on a windy day:

- ✔ **Put a windscreen over a stick microphone.** A windscreen (see Figure 8-6) looks like a little hat for your microphone. It cuts down on the whistle of the wind (as well as heavy breathing sounds, if your subject is winded).

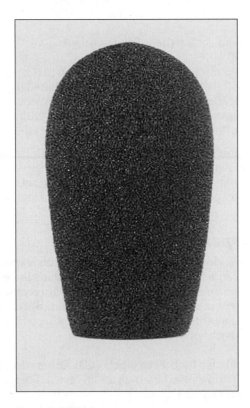

**Figure 8-6:** Windscreen.

✔ **Put a wind muff on your boom microphone.** From a distance, a boom microphone with a wind muff (see Figure 8-7) looks like a comatose squirrel dangling on a pole over the subject. But this woolly accessory can deal with some of the worst conditions and reduce noise by nearly 10 dB. The big problem is keeping it out of your shot.

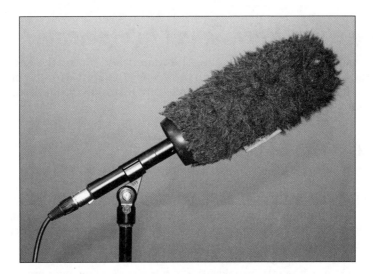

Figure 8-7: Wind muff over boom microphone.

✔ **Use a blimp.** A blimp comes in handy when conditions are really tough, such as when you're recording in a howling wind. This accessory is a big hollow tube that fits around the microphone and creates a pocket of stillness around it by absorbing wind vibrations.

## Staying close to the subject

If you're a fan of the classic television sitcom *Seinfeld,* you may be familiar with the episode "The Puffy Shirt," in which Jerry was asked to wear a puffy shirt by a low-talking fashion designer. Because he didn't hear what the low talker was actually asking him to do, he ended up wearing the shirt during a television appearance. He should have gotten closer to hear what she was saying.

The same applies to using a microphone. The closer the microphone is to the subject, the better the audience can understand his words, and the less likely you are to have extraneous noise polluting the audio track.

It's hard *not* to have the subject close to you when you're shooting with GoPro. If you're not using the GoPro's on-camera microphone as your primary audio source, use a shotgun microphone or a wireless model closer to the subject.

You may want to use a *pop screen,* which is a circular foam accessory stretched across a frame that clips in front of a microphone. Besides looking cool, this inexpensive attachment reduces *plosive* noises — the "pop" sounds in words beginning with *b, p,* or *t.* If you don't use a pop screen, the subject's plosives may be the vocal equivalents of fingernails on a chalkboard.

# Working with Other Sound Equipment

Somewhere between mounting the camera and hitting the Record button lies the awareness of the sound on the scene. You start with the procedural stuff, such as making sure the audio levels are just right. From there, you can use more elaborate sound tools.

## Using an audio line mixer

The GoPro lets you connect a microphone with a mini-plug (refer to "Adding a GoPro accessory microphone," earlier in this chapter). Professional-quality microphones use three-pin XLR cables. You can produce acceptable audio with a mini-plug microphone, but what happens when you want to use a higher-quality microphone or just plug the camera, via adapters, into a soundboard?

A portable line mixer makes the two types of mikes play nicely together. This relatively affordable accessory (see Figure 8-8) connects microphones to the camera and also connects the camera to a soundboard for optimal recording of events such as concerts, performances, and parties.

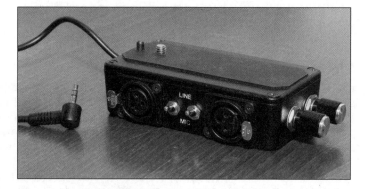

Figure 8-8: Portable line mixer.

The small, lightweight mixer lets you attach a professional XLR microphone or other audio signals to a camera that has a 3.5mm mini-plug microphone input. The mixer can upgrade and expand the audio capabilities of your GoPro to the level of a professional video camcorder. In addition, you can connect more than one microphone.

Most portable mixers let you select Line and Mic levels:

- ✔ **Line:** Line level creates a strong signal for transferring audio from a source such as an audio mixing board, as opposed to an external microphone.

- ✔ **Mic:** When you're using an external microphone, use this setting. Microphones don't require a high signal to record audio, and if you set the line mixer to Line, the sound will be loud and distorted.

## Using headphones

It's always a good idea to use headphones to monitor audio. You can not only hear when the sound overmodulates (that's a fancy way of saying it's distorted), but also listen for unwanted sounds and distortion.

Following are a few common types of headphones:

- ✔ **Earbuds:** The headphones you use with iOS devices can work with your DSLR. The audio quality is acceptable.

- ✔ **Ear pads:** These small, inexpensive, over-the-ear headphones are adequate, but they don't isolate ambient sound.

- ✔ **Clip-ons:** Clip-on headphones clip directly to your ears. They can come in handy, especially when you can use a clip-on that's clipped on one ear.

- ✔ **Full size:** Full-size headphones have large cups that cover your ears. These headphones are best for listening to music while relaxing in an easy chair — not for monitoring audio.

Noise-canceling headphones aren't recommended, because you need to pay attention to ambient sound.

# Part III
# Movies Are Made in Postproduction

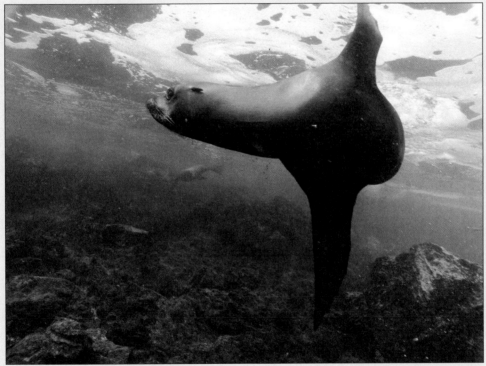

©istockphoto.com/naes Image #23259702

Find out how to get even more imaginative with GoPro Studio Edit at `www.dummies.com/extras/goprocameras`.

# In this part . . .

- ✔ Understand workstation requirements.
- ✔ Master the basics of GoPro Studio Edit.
- ✔ Make a GoPro-style video with templates.
- ✔ Add transitions and titles.
- ✔ Export your move for various uses.

# 9

# Equipping Your Edit Station

## In This Chapter

▶ Choosing a computer platform

▶ Knowing your workstation requirements

▶ Adding extra equipment

▶ Selecting video editing software

*T*echnology has come so far that "editing suite" often refers to your table of choice at your favorite coffee place with your laptop computer. You can literally put a movie together with headphones on while sipping your latte. You can sip a cappuccino when downloading footage from your camera and immediately start editing your movie. All it takes is a machine with enough horsepower — most consumer models have it these days — to run GoPro Studio Edit, or your favorite editing app.

Not all computers are created equal; some are clearly a little more robust when it comes to efficiently handling all that you throw at it. Often that difference comes down to having a faster processor and an abundance of RAM.

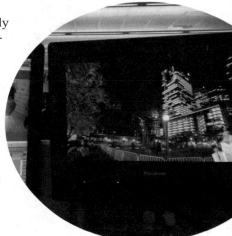

## Picking a Computer Platform

The rivalry between Macs and PCs used to have the same intensity as debates between Yankees and Mets fans or Ohio State and Michigan followers. Although the sports rivalries are still pretty intense, the one between Macs and PCs has softened a bit.

Both operating systems can help you achieve your goals; they just happen to go about the process differently. Chances are that the computer you already own can meet your video editing needs.

## Comparing operating systems

If you're on the fence about switching platforms or just want to validate your current choice as the right one for moviemaking, consider the operating systems:

- **Mac OS:** The latest incarnation of Mac OS is Mavericks, also known as OS 10.9. It offers improved performance, Finder enhancements, and iOS compatibility for greater communication with the iPhone and iPad.

- **Windows:** Windows 8 is the latest operating system for PC-based computers, providing advanced media support such as touch-screen functionality. A basic edition and three other configurations (Windows 8 Pro, Windows 8 Enterprise, and Windows RT) are available.

## Macintosh

Walk out of an Apple Store with a Mac, and you can start editing your movie not long after you take it out of the box, because iMovie is loaded on every Mac.

### Mac models

Currently, you can choose among these models:

- **MacBook Air:** This lightweight version of the MacBook, the MacBook Air sheds some weight and thickness by leaving out a DVD slot and conventional hard drive. It has less processor speed than its big brother, the MacBook Pro, but it's still adequate for video editing, especially when it's connected to a fast external hard drive.

- **MacBook Pro:** This powerful laptop lets you edit anywhere. It includes a SuperDrive for reading and burning media discs. It has Thunderbolt connectors and USB 3 inputs to connect to just about anything.

- **iMac series:** This popular all-in-one desktop computer acts as an edit station right out of the box. Like the MacBook Pro (see the preceding item), it has Thunderbolt connectors and USB 3 inputs.

- **Mac Pro:** The Big Kahuna of the Macintosh line, this tower computer offers enough raw power to edit a feature film with special effects, as well as process high-quality CGI animation. It's not light on the pocket, and the monitor and other peripherals are separate purchases, so for anyone who's just breaking into the field, it may be overkill. But it's a durable workhorse for serious moviemaking.

- **Mac mini:** The Mac mini is the powerful tiny version of the Mac Pro. As with the Pro, you add the monitor, keyboard, and mouse of your choice.

### Minimum editing requirements for a Mac

For optimum video editing, choose a Mac with these specs or better:

- Intel Dual Core processor
- Mac OS X 10.6.3 (Snow Leopard) or later
- 2GB of RAM
- Display resolution of 1280 x 768 pixels
- 5,400 rpm internal hard drive
- External hard drive with Thunderbolt, USB 3.0, or eSATA connectivity

## Windows

At entry level, Windows PCs are cheaper than Macs, though cost is significantly affected by component quality. These days, PCs have enough initial power to edit video, but they may not include a fast-enough hard drive or a complete set of connection types.

### PC models

Numerous manufacturers make PCs — including Dell, Toshiba, Hewlett-Packard (HP), and Sony — and each manufacturer makes several lines that use a variety of components. Even when you isolate your choice to laptops, you still have to consider differing screen sizes, processors, and connectivity arrays.

PC models come in the following types:

- **Desktop:** Better desktop PCs feature fast multicore processors, sound boards, multiple hard drives, and high-speed inputs.
- **Laptop:** Some models excel at high-definition (HD) video editing; others fall short. Check the specs for running GoPro before committing to a laptop. Standout models include the Sony Vaio Pro series and the Dell 7000 series.
- **All-in-one:** All-in-one PCs offers fast processing, HDMI connectivity, and large screens. Many models support video editing, including the Sony Vaio L Series and the HP Touchsmart.

### Minimum editing requirements for a PC

For best video editing performance, choose a Windows PC with these specs or better:

- Intel Core 2 Duo processor
- Windows XP with Service Pack 3, Windows Vista, or Windows 7

- 2GB of RAM
- Graphics card that supports OpenGL 1.2 or better
- Display resolution of 1280 x 800 pixels
- 5,400-rpm internal hard drive
- External drive with USB 3.0 or eSATA connectivity
- QuickTime 7.6 or later

## Understanding Workstation Requirements

When it comes to editing video, some computers are clearly better suited than others. Here's what you need for your moviemaking workstation.

### Newer computer

More often than not, older computers are more replaceable than upgradable. An older iMac that doesn't include at least a FireWire 800 connection, for example, won't be usable with a fast external hard disk. Neither will a Windows PC with a slow graphics card or a processor that can't run the latest operating system.

TECHNICAL STUFF

### Cashing in on the cache

The cache is perhaps the most-overlooked component in high-speed computing. Every time you do something on your computer, the processor gathers instructions to honor the request. The processor can execute actions faster than memory can, so it uses various levels of cache to accomplish tasks. Cache is a funny thing in that you don't always notice when it's there, but you know when it's not there.

Here's how cache helps in editing video:

- **Level 1 (L1) cache:** This type of cache speeds the editing process, but only in short bursts. It works harder when the processor needs a little help and then goes back to working

normally. Like eating a chocolate bar when you're hungry, using Level 1 cache is satisfying but not meant to replace the meal.

- **Level 2 (L2) cache:** At this level, a little more memory is available to crunch the data, but performance at this level is slightly slower than Level 1 cache.

- **Level 3 (L3) cache:** This level has more memory than Level 1 and Level 2 combined. Processing is slower than at those levels but significantly faster than RAM. A processor with an adequate L3 cache performs significantly faster than a computer with more RAM.

## Better-than-minimum speed

Editing HD video is serious business, so your computer's processor had better be up for the challenge. Whether you're using a new machine or an old one, be sure it exceeds the minimum requirements to run your editing software (see "Picking Software That Suits Your Needs" later in this chapter).

A processor has much in common with a drummer in a rock band: Each needs to keep up to do the job. When you capture 30 frames per second, the processor has to play 30 individual frames per second (fps) without missing a beat. Processing a continuous video signal is an arduous task, and any hitch or glitch can seriously slow the process or even drop frames.

## Large monitor

If you have a desktop computer, get the biggest screen you can afford. With a laptop, you're a bit limited, but try to get at least a 15-inch screen.

## Lots of RAM

Your computer can't live without random access memory (RAM), and you can never have enough of the stuff. It feeds your processor-hungry video editing software while updating your Facebook status. The more RAM you have, the better, and because HD movie files require a lot of memory, buy as much as you can afford. Fortunately, RAM is relatively cheap.

---

### Know your drives

Not all hard drives are created equal. Here are a few types of drives you're already using or can add to your system:

✔ **Internal drives:** The internal hard drive is the one that's already in your desktop or laptop computer. A basic one runs at 5,400 rpm, though some inexpensive computers use drives that run at 4,500 rpm.

✔ **External drives:** External hard drives are available in various flavors. Benefits include compatibility with various computers and faster access speed than internal drives can offer. Some external drives are self-powered to accommodate on-the-go editing needs.

✔ **RAID arrays:** A RAID (Random Array of Independent Disks) array is a group of hard drives connected to act as a single unit for increased performance and stability.

### Fast graphics card

Think of the graphics card as a specialist hired by the processor to reproduce the image and redraw the screen 30 times per second. Today, video is recorded and played back at 60 fps — and 120 fps and higher rates loom on the horizon. Your graphics card has its work cut out for it. Many computers built over the past couple of years are more than adequate to run GoPro Studio Edit.

## Accessorizing Your Station

Accessorizing your outfits makes good fashion sense, and so does adding accessories to your editing workstation. If you have room on your desk and in your budget, add a second monitor and some comfortable peripherals.

### Connecting an extra monitor

Your video footage and your video editing tools reside on the same monitor, so it's a good idea to connect another monitor to separate the editing tools from the actual video (see Figure 9-1). Also, adding a high-quality monitor helps with video quality control.

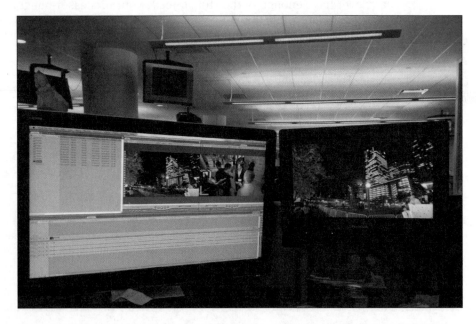

Figure 9-1: Professional-quality monitor connected to a Mac Pro running Final Cut Studio 2.

The hardest part about connecting a monitor is making sure that you have the proper connectors. Even if your computer doesn't have a dedicated video connection, you can connect another monitor via USB or Thunderbolt.

Set up the extra monitor as an extension or mirror of your main monitor, according to your needs:

- **Extending the monitor** adds more real estate by continuing the monitor on the other monitor. This arrangement is perfect for adding space to separate your editing tools from the video player. Extending gives you more room and allows you to multitask without overpopulating your screen.

- **Mirroring the monitor** is exactly what it sounds like. This technique is great for working on your main monitor while showing your work to an audience on the other monitor.

### Adding a monitor to a Mac

To set up an additional monitor on a Mac, make sure you have the right connector, and enjoy dual-screen bliss. Here's how:

1. **Connect the second monitor to the Mac, using the appropriate connector.**

   Use one of the following:

   - *Thunderbolt cable:* Transfers both data and a display signal.

   - *VGA adapter:* Lets you connect any standard analog monitor, projector, or LCD screen that uses a VGA connector.

   - *DVI adapter:* Allows you to connect a monitor that has a DVI connector.

   - *Mini monitor port to VGA adapter:* Lets you connect a second monitor to any Macintosh with a Thunderbolt port.

2. **Turn the monitor on.**

3. **Choose System Preferences from the Apple menu.**

4. **Select Monitors in the System Preferences window.**

   If you don't see it, select Detect Monitors.

5. **Adjust the resolution, colors, and refresh rate as desired.**

   If your Mac is running the Mavericks operating system, simply choose Best for Monitor.

6. **Specify how you want to use the second screen.**

   The default setting extends the screen between the two monitors. Rearrange the orientation of the monitors by dragging one over the other and clicking the Arrangement button. If you want both monitors to show the same screen image, select the Mirror Monitors check box.

### Adding a second monitor to a PC

Using another monitor with your Windows PC is simple. Follow these steps:

1. **Turn off the computer, if it isn't already off.**

2. **Connect the second monitor via the** DVI or VGA port.

3. **Turn the computer and the second monitor on.**

   The Windows operating system looks for both monitors. Don't be alarmed if the new monitor doesn't turn on.

4. **Activate the second monitor.**

   To do this:

   a. *Right-click any spot on the screen, and choose Screen Resolution from the shortcut menu.*

   b. *Click the Settings tab of the Properties dialog box, which displays two boxes to represent the two monitors.*

   c. *Right-click the second monitor, and choose Attached from the shortcut menu.*

   d. *Click Apply in the resulting dialog box.*

   After some churning, the second monitor should come on.

5. **Specify what you want the monitors to do.**

   If you want to extend the video across the two monitors, for example, select the second monitor and select Extend these Displays.

## Adding ergonomic peripherals

Be sure to pick the keyboard and mouse that work for you. Some manufacturers make keyboards designed for specific nonlinear editing programs, such as Apple Final Cut X and Adobe Premiere CS.

### Keyboarding bliss

Maybe it's not as much fun as snowboarding — especially if you love strapping a board to your feet and negotiating a snowy hill — but there's something incredibly pleasurable about using the right keyboard. Whether you like one that has a specific action or helps with your repetitive-stress injury, it's key (pun intended) to select the right one.

Although the keyboard that came with your computer does the job, you may want to upgrade to one of the following:

- ✓ **Dedicated editing keyboard:** With color-coded keys and written instructions, this keyboard (see Figure 9-2) familiarizes you with editing shortcuts. Also, it looks pretty cool on your desk.

- ✓ **Ergonomic keyboard:** An ergonomic keyboard is designed to provide a more natural feel when typing and to reduce injury.

- ✓ **Wireless keyboard:** A wireless keyboard frees a USB connection on your computer and allows you to move the keyboard without tangling cables.

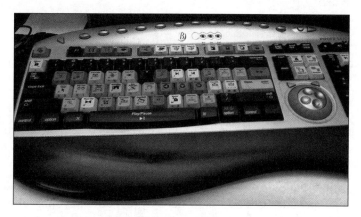

**Figure 9-2:** Dedicated keyboard for editing in Final Cut Studio.

### *Sometimes a mouse is not a rodent*

This popular peripheral got its name because it resembled a mouse with a tail. These days, you'd be hard-pressed to find a mouse with a tail: Most modern mice are wireless. Some pointing devices aren't even mice; they're trackpads or trackballs.

For video editing, it's common to use a shuttle control. As an active part of video editing process, it guides you through the program interface and the timeline with relative ease.

# Picking Software That Suits Your Needs

Many novices think that their unedited video footage stands on its own. It's possible to understand an unedited clip of some specific action, but that case is more the exception than the rule. But more often, raw footage doesn't satisfy anyone but the person who shot it.

For that reason, it's important to edit your footage with a nonlinear editing program. Which one? You have a lot of programs to choose among, and all of them do pretty much the same thing, so you may want to base your decision on your needs and budget.

Occasionally, problems arise when you use video editing software on an older computer, depending on how old the computer is and what version of the operating system it uses. Check the system requirements of the software you're considering.

## Free software

You can download GoPro Studio Edit *gratis,* but you may already have a pretty decent moviemaking program on your Mac or Windows PC.

### GoPro Studio Edit

For many of your needs, you may not have to go further than GoPro Studio Edit (see Figure 9-3). The software is free to download — and more important, it's designed to work with GoPro cameras.

GoPro Studio Edit is packed with features, including a series of templates that allow you to produce GoPro-style videos by just adding your video to appropriate places. I discuss this software in more detail in Chapter 10.

GoPro Studio Edit doesn't discriminate and works well with both Windows PCs and Macs. Computers running Windows XP, Vista, Windows 8 Pro, Windows 8 Enterprise, and Windows RT can all run the software. So can any Mac running OS X 10.6.3 or later.

### iMovie

Standard issue on Macintosh computers for more than a decade, iMovie (see Figure 9-4) is a popular choice among amateur video editors. It offers many special effects and fully integrates with Mac programs such as iTunes and iPhoto. Although the software is easy to use and loaded with functions and themes, some people may find it limited for advanced editing.

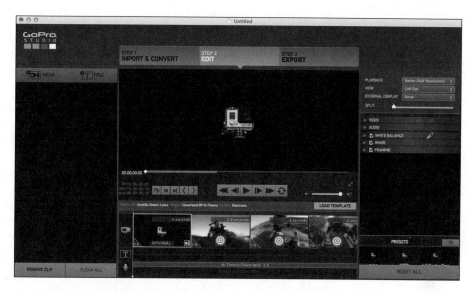

Figure 9-3: GoPro Studio Edit.

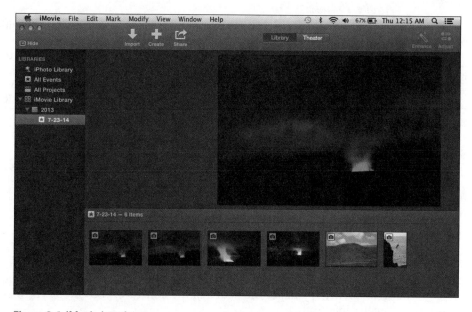

Figure 9-4: iMovie interface.

### Windows Movie Maker

Included on most Windows PCs, this powerful little program lets you make movies easily. It's intuitive to use and includes many fun effects.

## Paid software

GoPro Studio Edit provides a great starting point for creating your movie, but it's not the only game in town. More elaborate programs are available that go beyond GoPro Studio Edit.

### Final Cut Pro

Considered by many people to be the de facto standard for nonlinear editing, Final Cut Pro appeals to the prosumer market. Robust, powerful, and filled with every imaginable function, this video editing program lets you do anything your creative heart can dream up. It captures or transfers video files in just about any format and exports them with a great deal of flexibility.

On the down side, Final Cut Pro works only on Macs.

### Adobe Premiere Pro

One of the oldest nonlinear editing programs on the market, Premiere has a devoted following. It helps you edit professional-quality movies, and it integrates nicely with the Adobe programs After Effects and Photoshop. Native DSLR editing presets in the newest version make it ideal for creative GoPro moviemaking. The software runs smoothly on both Macs and Windows PCs. Just make sure that your workstation has enough RAM and a decent graphics card.

### Adobe Premiere Elements

This abridged version of Premiere Pro (see the preceding section) is not only affordable, but also powerful. Version 11 includes a wide range of new features. It behaves the same way on a Macintosh as it does on a Windows PCs.

### Sony Vegas Pro Movie Studio

If you're looking for affordable video editing software that lets you edit pro-quality movies, there are worse choices than Vegas. Designed for the professional on the go, it includes a healthy selection of effects and 3-D capability to boot. When you get the knack of the software, you can use it to crank out quality material.

This program isn't available for the Mac.

### Pinnacle Studio HD

Another name synonymous with video editing, this consumer-level program offers a nice set of features. Don't expect it to have lots of bells and whistles, but what it does have ensures that you can make a successful movie. It's quite complex for an inexpensive program.

Macintosh users need not apply; Pinnacle Studio HD is strictly a Windows program.

# Getting Familiar with GoPro Studio Edit

*D*epending on when you grew up, the movies of your childhood (or perhaps of your child) may seem to have something in common: The camera ran too long for the movie to maintain its pizzazz. Sometimes, it took too long for the action to happen; at other times, the camera kept recording after the interesting stuff was done. More than likely, there just wasn't a whole lot of interesting content. The reason doesn't matter, because the result is the same: People are reluctant to watch.

The problem isn't necessarily shooting too much footage. Often, when you leave the camera running, you capture amazing activity. You never want to shoot less — maybe more wisely, but never less. As Tarzan might say, "Shooting lot of footage, good. Playing all that footage at family party, bad."

Editing your movie before showing it to anyone is always a good idea. By assembling the best pieces into a shorter, more concise movie, you not only hold your audience's attention, but also tell a story.

Using an intuitive editing program like GoPro Studio Edit provides some power to transform your clips into a cohesive, well-edited movie. When you've shot the footage, it's time to get to work. Unlike mowing the lawn or cleaning the gutters, this task is creative and thought-provoking.

For the section on GoPro Studio Edit, a Macintosh computer was used. Versions for both platforms are similar in operation.

# Why Use GoPro Studio Edit?

It's unlikely that anyone ever said, "Hey, I want to spend more money than necessary for some video editing software." That's like asking the Internal Revenue Service whether you can pay more taxes than you owe. But that's often what happens when beginners buy software that's too advanced.

These days, many affordable consumer programs are available, as mentioned in Chapter 9, but there's something nice about a free program. It's even nicer when that program is powerful and intuitive too. That's what you can expect from GoPro Studio Edit, which makes it easy to create professional-quality videos from your GoPro content. By providing features that specifically address that type of camera, the program lets you add effects and titles to your movie, as well as add voiceovers, music, and sound effects.

In addition, it includes a series of templates (influenced by popular GoPro videos) that accelerate the process of transforming your clips into an incredible movie.

Although GoPro is up to the task of working as a stand-alone program, you can also integrate it with other, more powerful nonlinear editing programs such as Apple's Final Cut Pro and Adobe Premiere.

## Seeing what's special about the program

Besides being free, GoPro Studio Edit offers the right amount of versatility. Here are some advantages of using this program:

- Intuitive working environment
- Nice selection of special-effects features
- Easy integration of clips recorded at different resolutions and frame rates with no visual loss of quality
- Variety of templates
- Capability to export a high-quality master file with up to 4K resolution for broadcast or archival purposes
- Capability to export projects as H.264 MP4 files at up to 1080p resolution for sharing on sites such as YouTube and Vimeo.

## Getting the software on your computer

Editing your GoPro footage for free is just a few clicks away when you download the software from the GoPro site.

Besides the free version, two paid versions of the software are available: GoPro Studio Edit Premium and GoPro Studio Edit Professional.

Before you get the software, make sure that your computer meets the minimum requirements mentioned in Chapter 9. If your computer is good to go, you're ready to start downloading. Follow these steps:

1. **Go to** `http://gopro.com`, **click the Products link, and navigate to the software page.**

2. **Choose your operating system from the drop-down menu.**

3. **Enter your email address.**

4. **Click the Download button.**

5. **When the** `.dmg` **(Mac) or** `.exe` **(Windows) file finishes downloading to your computer, double-click it to open the installer.**

6. **Double-click the installer icon.**

7. **Follow the installation wizard's prompts.**

# Breaking Down the Interface

GoPro Studio Edit 2 offers a new, user-friendly interface with lots of controls and features.

The player window (see Figure 10-1) provides three panes:

- **Import & Convert:** This pane is where you import your files into the program and convert source files to the CineForm format. (I discuss CineForm in Chapter 11.)

- **Edit:** In this pane, you put the movie together, doing everything from trimming clips to adding effects, titles, and music.

- **Export:** This pane provides the necessary tools to convert your movie to a self-playing movie file.

The window's function depends on what you're working with in the program:

- **Individual clips in the Media Bin:** Click a clip in the Media Bin, and it loads it in the player. Press the play button to view it. You can trim the clip by setting in and out points (see Figure 10-2).

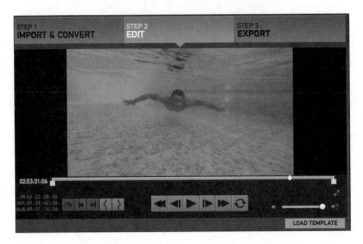

Figure 10-1: The three panes of the player window.

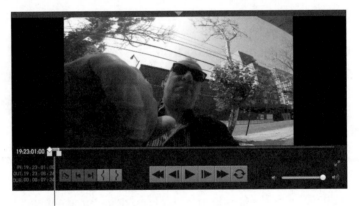

In and out points

Figure 10-2: Player window showing a clip with in and out points.

- ✔ **Clips on the Storyboard:** If you click the Storyboard, the clips play in order.
- ✔ **Individual clip on the Storyboard:** More than likely, your Storyboard is populated with clips. Double-click a clip to play it. You can also trim a clip.

## Deciphering the menus

Navigating the features of GoPro Studio Edit is similar to driving to a friend's house a few towns away, as opposed to navigating bigger, more complicated programs, which is like driving cross-country. You still have to know the lay of the land, though. In this section, I cover the menus and their commands. The Mac and PC versions are similar in operation, although the Mac version has more operations under the menus.

### File menu

The commands on this menu let you create a project, import content, and save the project:

- **New Project:** As you might expect, this command creates a new project.

- **Open Project:** This command lets you navigate to a project you've already started.

- **Open Recent Project:** This command displays a submenu of projects you've already started.

- **Match Stereo Pair (Mac only):** This command combines multiple audio channels into a single stereo file.

- **Import Media (Mac only):** Choose this command to locate and import into GoPro Studio Edit.

- **Load GoPro Template:** This command allows you to select a template for your movie.

- **Close:** This command does exactly what it says to the file you have open.

- **Save Project:** This command saves your project and prompts you for a filename if you're saving it for the first time.

- **Save Project As:** The Save Project As command, which lets you change the project name when saving, comes in handy when you want to have an alternative project name.

- **Revert to Saved (Mac only):** Choose this command if you've made a lot of wild changes since the last time you saved the project and want to get back to that point.

### Edit menu

The commands in this menu include many of those that you normally find on Edit menus. They are

- **Undo:** This command lets you reverse your last 50 actions. You could choose the menu command 50 times, or press ⌘+Z (Mac) or Ctrl+Z (Windows) 50 times and then erase those steps.

- **Redo:** Just in case you've undone too much, this command allows you to start bringing everything back.

- **Cut (Mac only):** The Cut command removes a Storyboard element and copies it the clipboard, just in case you change your mind.

- ✓ **Copy:** This command lets you copy an element for future use and holds it in the clipboard.

- ✓ **Paste:** The Paste command moves a copied or cut element to a new place.

- ✓ **Clear Storyboard:** This command clears the Storyboard of all content.

- ✓ **Reset All:** Choose this command to clear any changes you made in the clip on the Storyboard.

### View menu (Mac Only)

Things get a little more interesting on the View menu:

- ✓ **Enter Full Screen:** The floating screen takes over the entire screen when you choose this command.

- ✓ **Play/Pause:** This command is a toggle, allowing you to play and pause a clip wherever it resides: the Import Bin, Media Bin, or Storyboard.

- ✓ **Stop:** Stop stops the movie.

- ✓ **Fast Rewind:** This command rewinds clips quickly, allowing you to look for a specific point in the footage.

- ✓ **Fast Forward:** This command does the same thing as Fast Rewind, only in reverse.

- ✓ **Previous Edit Point:** This command moves the Storyboard time indicator to the last clip on the Storyboard.

- ✓ **Next Edit Point:** This command moves the Storyboard time indicator to the next clip on the Storyboard.

- ✓ **Mark In:** Choose this command to set the point where the clip should begin before trimming.

- ✓ **Mark Out:** Choose this command to set the point where the clip should end before trimming.

- ✓ **Step Reverse:** This command moves backward through the Storyboard or selected clip.

- ✓ **Step Forward:** This command moves forward through the Storyboard or selected clip.

- ✓ **Split:** Choose this command to divides the selected clip.

- ✓ **Loop Playback:** This command makes the Storyboard or selected clip repeat until you intervene.

### Share menu (Mac only)

Sparse in choices, the Share menu offers two choices for exporting your movie or still image:

✔ **Export Movie:** Lets you export the movie. The resulting Export Movie dialog box provides resolution and format options (see Chapter 11).

✔ **Export Still:** Allows you to export a still frame from the movie in three file sizes, as well as in the native format.

### Window menu (Mac only)

The Window menu contains commands that have to do with the program window and its relationship to the computer screen:

✔ **Minimize:** This command hides GoPro Studio Edit so you can see other open programs on your computer.

✔ **Zoom:** This command fills the screen with the program.

✔ **Show Conversion Details:** This command shows the conversion setting of the selected clip.

✔ **Bring All to Front:** If you're running other applications while you're editing in GoPro Studio Edit, this command allows you to bring GoPro to the front.

### Help menu

Rounding out the menus is Help:

✔ **Search (Mac only):** Choose this command, and type a topic you're trying to find information on.

✔ **GoPro Studio Manual:** This command accesses the manual.

✔ **Online Support:** This command launches web-based help.

✔ **Tutorial:** Choose this command to find the appropriate tutorial for what you're doing, such as Import, Edit, or Export.

✔ **Device Window:** This command lets you update your GoPro camera and other accessories.

# Bringing in Media

I'm sure you're familiar with the fable of rubbing a magic lamp and having a genie pop up to grant you three wishes. There's no genie in GoPro Studio Edit, but the first time you try to import content, a tutorial on importing pops up (see Figure 10-3).

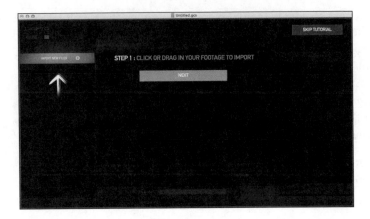

Figure 10-3: The Import tutorial.

Alternatively, you can choose this tutorial from the Help menu.

With or without a tutorial, it's easy to import your GoPro footage and any other elements you want to add.

## Importing media from your GoPro

Downloading image and movie files from your GoPro is easy. Just plug the camera into the computer's USB port. Then you can do the following:

- **Import files through GoPro Studio Edit.** Click the Import New Files button at the top of the player window's Import & Convert pane. An import dialog box opens. Select the DCIM folder, and click Open. You can also access the folder where the movie resides and choose the files you want, if you don't feel like opening the entire batch.

- **Pull the files off the camera.** Navigate to the DCIM folder and drag the files from the camera to the desktop.

- **Use another app.** Mac users can easily open files through iPhoto or iMovie. On a PC, you can grab files from Movie Maker or Photo.

## Importing other media files

If you want to add footage from other sources to your GoPro movie, you can easily import clips from your camcorder or other camera. Just connect that device to your computer via the USB port, click the Import New Files button at the top of the Import & Convert pane, use the Import New Files dialog box to navigate to the media you want to import, and click Open. This process works for audio files, too.

# Using GoPro Edit Templates

At one point or another, a co-worker or friend may have pulled you aside to show you some cool GoPro video online. Guess what? Now you can make your own. GoPro Studio Edit offers templates based on the most popular GoPro videos to transform your footage into another exciting GoPro video.

The program comes with four templates (see Figure 10-4):

- ✔ **Dubstep Baby:** Slow-motion video and dubstep music can transform your baby video into a hip clip.

- ✔ **Laser Cats:** There's no shortage of cat-video fans on the Internet, so it seems like a no-brainer to combine your cat with GoPro video and a cool layout. All you need to do is drop in your own cat video, and away you go.

- ✔ **Ocotillo Desert Lines:** The action-movie template lets you add your own exciting video to produce a nicely constructed segment.

- ✔ **Pool Party with the Niños:** Replace this family with your family for an impressive movie.

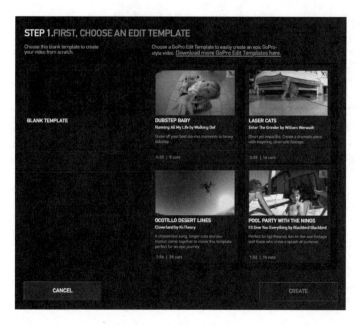

Figure 10-4: Pick a template.

Other templates are available online. To download more templates for free, go to `http://gopro.com/studio-templates-download?referral=studio_app&version`.

Just follow these steps to create a video by using a GoPro template:

1. **Choose File⇨Load Edit Template.**

   The Browse Edit Templates dialog box opens.

2. **Select a template.**

   The template you choose populates the Storyboard, providing sample video clips, music, and titles. Each template lists the title, artist and song, a brief description, duration, number of clips used, and tempo.

3. **Replace the content of the template with your own.**

   Just drag the new footage to the target on the clip in the Storyboard. Repeat it for other clips you want to include.

4. **Save and export your movie.**

# Implementing an Efficient Workflow

Everyone has different needs, but some basic practices will make your time using GoPro Studio Edit swift and productive.

## Customizing your workspace

GoPro Studio Edit doesn't offer a lot of preferences or settings, so you can't customize for all your needs. Think of it as being like the computer at the office that everyone shares: It works well, but you wouldn't dare use your vacation pictures as a screen saver. Well, it's the same thing when using GoPro Studio Edit. You can't adjust the size of your bins and windows or create your own keyboard shortcuts, but that doesn't mean you can't use it as an effective tool.

## Organizing projects and files

It's essential to organize your movie content to make the process go as smoothly as possible. Here are a few things you can do:

- **Group your visual assets.** Put all the visuals you want to use in your movies inside a folder so you can access them easily.

- **Create a project folder.** This folder keeps your GoPro movies in the same place. It differs from your visual-assets folder, which acts more like a storage area.

✔ **Name your folders consistently.** Using a coherent naming convention for folders will help you find footage six months from now.

✔ **Import only what you need.** There's no sense in filling the program with excessive footage, especially if you have no intention of using it. Keep things lean and mean.

## Setting preferences

If having the fewest preferences were a competition, GoPro Studio Edit would be a finalist. The Preferences dialog box (see Figure 10-5) offers a limited number of options:

✔ **Use Time of Day for Timecode:** This option takes the time of day from the source file and writes it into the time-code track of the converted file.

✔ **Use Reel Name in Destination:** This option lets you name the clip that you're converting.

✔ **Auto-Start Conversions:** This option automatically starts converting files when they're added to the Conversion List (see Chapter 11).

✔ **AutoSave Is On:** When this option is selected, the project is saved automatically at the intervals you set, which range from 30 seconds to 60 minutes.

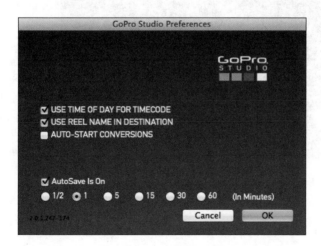

Figure 10-5: The GoPro Studio Preferences dialog box.

# Delving Deeper into GoPro Studio Edit

Every section of the program windows contains its own controls. In this section, I review them to help you master the program.

## Navigating the player window's controls

GoPro Studio Edit is like the Swiss Army knife of video editing programs. It's a bit scaled down when compared to programs like Final Cut Pro and Adobe Premiere, but it still provides you enough tools to get the job done, minus the small saw and fold-out scissors. The program's features and functions center around the player window, which has three states that show different features depending on what you're doing in the program. Here is a brief description.

### Import & Convert pane

The Import & Convert pane (also known as the Import Room; see Figure 10-6) is where you import your movie clips, trim the footage, and choose advanced conversion settings.

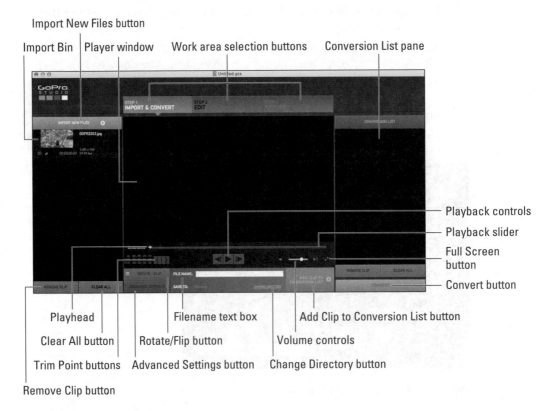

Figure 10-6: The Import & Convert pane.

Following are brief descriptions of the pane's controls:

- ✔ **Import:** Click this button to bring media into the program. (Alternatively, choose File⇨Import.)

- ✔ **Import Bin:** The Import Bin holds the media you've imported for the project.

- ✔ **Playback slider:** This slider shows the progress of the clip or movie, both in the position of playhead and the time code.

- ✔ **Playhead:** This diamond-shaped icon shows the progress of the clip playing. Drag it to scroll through the clip.

- ✔ **Remove Clip:** Click this button to delete a clip from the Import Bin.

- ✔ **Clear All:** Click this button to remove all clips from the Import Bin.

- ✔ **Rotate/Flip:** Click this button to rotate or flip the selected clip.

- ✔ **Advanced Conversion settings:** These controls let you modify the image size, frame rate, and quality. In addition, you can speed the clip or apply a motion blur.

- ✔ **Trim Point:** Click this button to set in and out points to trim your source file.

- ✔ **Filename text box:** Enter the name of each clip here.

- ✔ **Playback controls:** These controls let you play the clip, as well as play it frame-by-frame in forward or reverse.

- ✔ **Change Directory:** Click this button to change the directory in which the clip will be saved.

- ✔ **Add to Conversion List:** Click this button to add the file in the player to the Conversion List.

- ✔ **Convert All:** Click this button to convert everything in the Import Bin.

- ✔ **Full Screen:** Click this button to make GoPro Studio Edit fill the screen. Press the Escape key on your keyboard, and it reverts to the floating window.

- ✔ **Volume controls:** These controls allow you to adjust the volume.

### Edit pane

The Edit pane (see Figure 10-7) is where you take the edit to the next level. You can add effects, music, and titles, as well as combine multiple videos on a Storyboard. Access it by clicking the second tab at the top of the player window.

Remove Clip button

Media Bin

Add Media button    Add Title button

Color Correction, Framing, and 3D controls

Global Playback controls

Volume controls

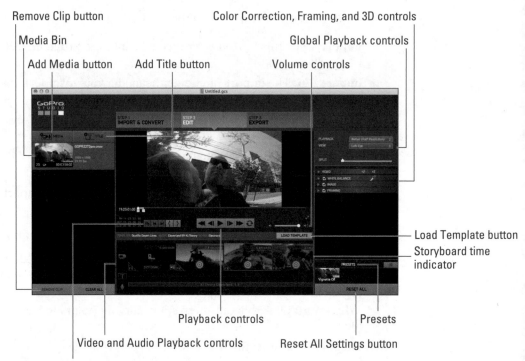

Load Template button

Storyboard time indicator

Playback controls

Presets

Video and Audio Playback controls

Reset All Settings button

Trim, Split, and Clip Navigation controls

**Figure 10-7:** The Edit pane.

Here are the controls in this pane:

- **Add Media:** Click this button to add converted media files to your project for editing.

- **Add Title:** Click this button to bring up a box where you can type a title and adjust its font, size, and style.

- **Media Bin:** This area contains the converted media clips.

- **Remove Clip:** Click this button to delete clips from the Media Bin.

- **Storyboard time indicator:** This control shows the duration of the move as it plays.

- **Volume controls:** Use these controls to adjust the volume.

- **Trim, Split, and Clip Navigation controls:** Use these tools to work on the clip.

- **Playback controls:** Use these tools to play the movie, scroll through the footage, and make frame-by-frame adjustments in forward and reverse.

- ✓ **Load Template:** Click this button to load one of the GoPro templates (refer to "Using GoPro Edit Templates" earlier in this chapter).

- ✓ **Global Playback controls:** These tools apply playback and view settings to the entire movie, as opposed to a single clip.

- ✓ **Video & Audio Playback controls:** These tools let you change a single clip rather than the entire movie.

- ✓ **Color Correction, Framing, and 3D controls:** These nested controls let you adjust white balance, exposure, cropping, and other settings.

- ✓ **Presets:** These controls let you apply image effects to your clips.

- ✓ **Reset All Settings:** Click this button to revert to the last-saved state after you change a clip.

### Export pane

You use the Export pane (see Figure 10-8) when your movie is complete. This pane offers only a few controls, which allow you to name the file, choose an export format, and save your movie in the appropriate folder.

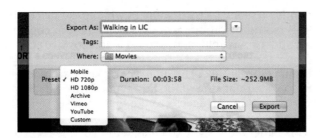

**Figure 10-8:** The Export pane.

## Making transitions

GoPro Studio Edit offer only one transition: a *dissolve*, where one scene slowly transforms into another. As long as you have two clips, you can add a dissolve. There's no menu command for this feature, and it's rather subtle, so if you blink, you can miss it.

To add a transition, follow these steps:

1. **Click the Edit pane to select it and display your Storyboard.**

2. **Click the Add Transition icon between two clips.**

   This icon is a tiny plus sign (+) resting on the yellow line between the clips (see Figure 10-9). The playhead does not have to be on the clip.

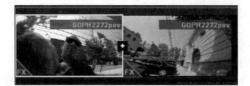

Figure 10-9: To create a dissolve, click the + sign.

3. **Set the duration of the dissolve.**

   When you click the + sign, you see a narrow box outlined in yellow that stretches across the two clips you set the dissolve.

4. **Click the Dissolve icon to select it.**

5. **Move the playhead to the desired out point on the playback slider.**

6. **Click the Mark Out button to shorten the duration of the dissolve.**

## Working with audio

Great audio depends on many factors, some of which take place during the editing phase. GoPro Studio Edit offers you a fair amount of control of audio. You can fix noise, add a sound effect, or record a voiceover track.

To access the audio controls, select a clip in the Storyboard and then click the Audio control on the right side of the Edit pane. The control panel shown in Figure 10-10 opens, giving you access to the following settings:

✓ **Level dB:** This slider allows you to change the volume level of the clip during playback. You can increase the level for clips with lower audio and decrease it for clips that are too loud or distorted. If you need to reset the levels, just click Level dB.

## Make sure your have enough frames

For the dissolve to work, you must have enough frames at the end of the first clip as well as at the start of the second one; otherwise, there's nothing to dissolve. If you plan to add dissolves, be sure the clip has the necessary frames. Also, the length of the dissolve cannot exceed the duration of the shortest clip. So if your first clip has an extra minute of footage that you trimmed in the Storyboard, but the second clip only has ten extra frames, then that's the longest you can make the dissolve.

✔ **Fade In:** This slider gradually raises audio level from silence.

✔ **Fade Out:** This slider gradually lowers the audio level to silence.

✔ **Completely Disable Audio from Video Clip:** Click the Audio Mute button on the clip's thumbnail.

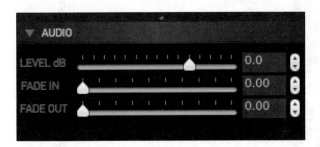

Figure 10-10: The Audio control panel.

## *Using a second video display*

You can use a second video monitor with GoPro Studio Edit. If you have one connected to your computer, the program recognizes it. Control this function through the Global Settings panel of the Edit pane (see Figure 10-11).

GoPro Studio Edit makes it easy to edit 3D video, especially when it comes to including a second monitor. You can still view your normal 2D files, but many of the options are for monitoring a 3D movie.

Following are brief descriptions of the options:

✔ **None:** The default setting means you aren't using a second monitor.

✔ **Left Eye:** This option shows the left-eye side of a 3D clip.

When you're working with 2D clips, always choose the Left Eye option for playback on a second monitor. If you don't have a secondary monitor, choose None.

✔ **Right Eye:** This option shows only the right-eye side of a 3D clip.

✔ **Anaglyph:** There are several Anaglyph settings:

- *Red/Cyan* shows the left and right eye tinted for viewing with red and cyan 3D glasses.

- *Red/Cyan/BW* shows the left and right eye in black-and-white and tinted for viewing with red/cyan 3D glasses.

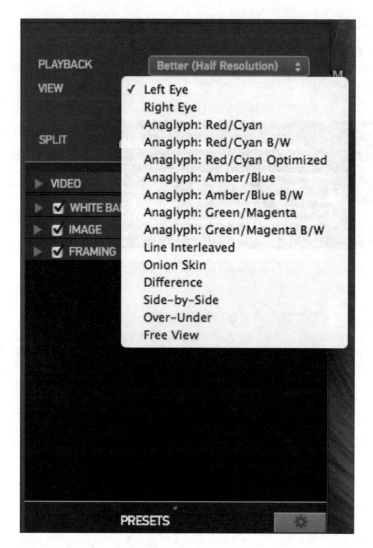

Figure 10-11: The Global Settings panel.

- *Red/Cyan/Optimized* shows the left and right eye tinted for optimal viewing with red/cyan 3D glasses.

- *Amber/Blue* shows the left and right eye tinted for viewing with amber/blue 3D glasses.

- *Amber/Blue/BW* shows the left and right eye in black-and-white and tinted for viewing with amber/blue 3D glasses.

- *Green/Magenta* shows the left and right eye tinted for viewing with green/magenta 3D glasses.

- *Green/Magenta/BW* shows the left and right eye in black-and-white and tinted for viewing with green/magenta 3D glasses.

✔ **Line Interleaved:** This option shows the left and right eye by alternating between horizontal lines and is used for certain polarized, passive 3D displays and polarized glasses.

✔ **Side-by-Side:** This option, for 3D monitors, shows side-by-side 3D mode on a second monitor.

✔ **Over-Under:** This option, used on 3D monitors, stacks the left and right eye and scales them vertically into one frame.

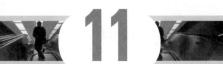

# Editing with GoPro Studio Edit

*In This Chapter*

▶ Creating a project

▶ Importing media

▶ Assembling the clips

▶ Getting audio levels right

▶ Using titles

**H**ave you ever wondered why your favorite movies ended up being your favorites? Maybe you liked the subject matter or an actor, but often it's because the movie was tightly structured.

Regardless of how well a movie is planned and shot, success comes from the editing process. Whether it's a studio blockbuster, a quaint indie film, or a student project, a well-edited movie compels viewers to escape into the world created onscreen. Conversely, a carelessly arranged film evokes negative emotions. Side effects may include drowsiness, indifference, and nausea.

Making compelling movies sounds like a monumental task, but it's entirely possible to succeed when you adhere to the fundamentals. This chapter covers the basics of editing a movie in GoPro Studio Edit.

## Creating Your Movie Project

Gathering all the assets for your movie can mean anything from putting the video, photos, and music in a folder ahead of time to downloading the day's shoot into GoPro Studio Edit. First, though, you have to create and save a new project. Next, you transfer your footage from the camera to your computer. Then it's time to bring the footage into GoPro Studio Edit.

## Starting a new project

To create a new project, follow these steps:

1. **Launch GoPro Studio Edit.**

   If you're using the program for the first time, a tutorial pop ups, offering some basic information on how to get files into the program. You can follow it if you want, but importing is pretty simple, so feel free to click the Skip Tutorial button.

   When you start GoPro you can get right to work because it creates a project by default.

2. **Choose File⇨New Project.**

   A new, blank project opens (see Figure 11-1).

Import New Files button

Import Bin          Import & Convert button          Conversion List pane

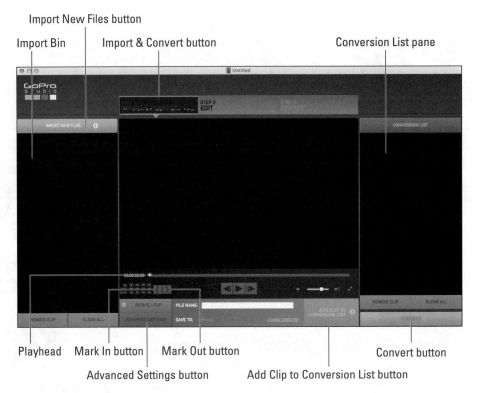

Playhead    Mark In button          Mark Out button                    Convert button

Advanced Settings button          Add Clip to Conversion List button

Figure 11-1: A new project.

3. **Choose File⇨Save Project to save the project.**

    Alternatively, press ⌘+S (Mac) or Ctrl+S (Windows).

4. **Navigate to your desired save folder.**

5. **Type a name for your project in the Filename text box.**

6. **Click the Save button.**

    The project is saved with the .gcs file extension.

## Importing video files

When you've created and named the project, you can fill it with content. To import a video file, follow these steps:

1. **Click the Import New Files button on the left side of the project window (refer to Figure 11-1).**

2. **Navigate to the folder that contains the files you want to import.**

3. **Select the desired file, and click Open.**

    The file loads in the Import Bin.

You can import an entire folder of clips at the same time by navigating to where it resides on your computer and dragging the folder from a window to the Import Bin.

### Importing and converting GoPro media

If you want to edit footage from your GoPro camera, you need to convert it to the CineForm *codec* (a program that compresses and decompresses files) before you can edit it into GoPro Studio Edit. That's because GoPro files are so compressed, converting them to CineForm is the only way to get them to play without lagging or dropping frames.

To import and convert GoPro footage for use in GoPro Studio Edit, follow these steps:

1. **Click the Import & Convert work area selection button in GoPro Studio Edit.**

2. **Click the Import New Files button in the top-left corner of the project window (refer to Figure 11-1).**

    The footage loads in the Import Bin.

3. **Click the Add Clip to Conversion List button in the bottom-right corner of the player window.**

4. **Click the Convert button (Convert All on a PC) in the bottom-right corner of the project window.**

   Conversion takes a few moments, depending on the length of the file. When conversion is complete, the file appears in the Conversion List pane (see Figure 11-2).

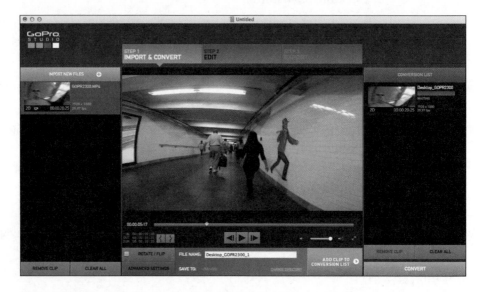

Figure 11-2: Converted files show up in the Conversion List.

### Adjusting fish-eye distortion

Capturing footage with the GoPro's ultra-wide-lens may have charm, but (as with eating chocolate cake or watching television) moderation is important. The fish-eye distortion produced by the lens can be interesting (see Figure 11-3), but a little less distortion sometimes makes it look better.

Here's how to make the fish-eye effect less extreme after you import footage into GoPro Studio Edit:

1. **Select the clip in the Conversion List pane (refer to Figure 11-3).**

2. **Click the Advanced Settings button in the bottom-left corner of the player window.**

3. **In the Advanced Settings dialog box, select Remove Fisheye.**

4. **Click OK.**

   After you convert the clip, the image has less distortion (see Figure 11-4).

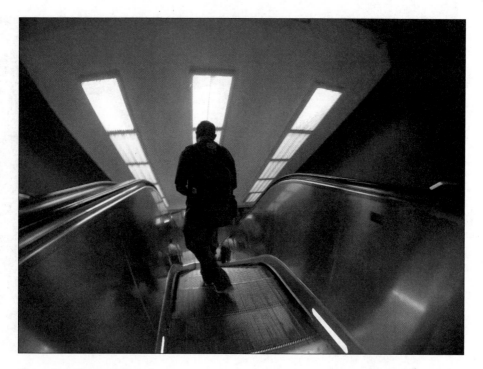

**Figure 11-3:** Fish-eye distortion.

## Viewing file information

When you import files, they appear as thumbnails in the Import Bin on the left side of the project window. Each thumbnail also contains some helpful file details (see Figure 11-5).

These details include

- **Filename:** You can change the name when you convert the file, if that's how you set your preferences (see Chapter 10).
- **Image size:** Knowing the resolution comes in handy when you shoot in both high definition (HD) and 4K.
- **Frame rate:** The frame rate of the clip is helpful when you have multiple clips with different settings.
- **2D or 3D:** This item is pretty self-explanatory.
- **Video or Time-Lapse icon:** This icon is informative when you shoot the same scene both ways.
- **Duration:** It's always nice to know the running time of a clip.

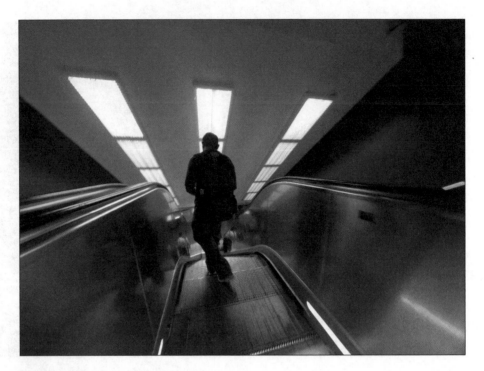

Figure 11-4: The image is less distorted.

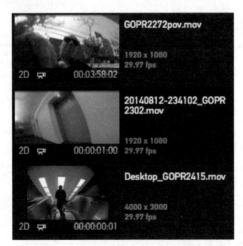

Figure 11-5: File details can be very helpful when you're selecting clips in a densely populated Import Bin.

## Viewing clips

You can select files in the Import Bin by clicking them. Press the up- and down-arrow keys on your keyboard to cycle through clips, or drag the playhead on the playback slider. You can play a clip by clicking it or by highlighting it and then clicking the Play button. Click the Step Forward and Step Backwards buttons to step through a clip one frame at a time.

When you're previewing your files, don't be surprised if you see choppy video. Choppy video is normal because the files are not yet converted to the CineForm codec. Depending on camera settings and the computer you're using to edit the movie, the effect will vary. But this is only for viewing; you cannot edit the clip until you convert it. You can, however, set in and out points so you only convert the parts of the clip you want to use.

## Deleting clips

More than likely, you won't want to use every clip you import. To remove a clip, select it and then click the Remove Clip button in the bottom-left corner of the Import Bin (refer to Figure 11-1), or select the clip and then press the Delete key on your keyboard.

To remove all clips at the same time, click the Clear All button in the bottom-right corner of the Import Bin.

# Putting the Pieces Together in the Edit Pane

Video editing is similar to assembling a jigsaw puzzle; there are lots of pieces, and it's up to you to make them fit. But movie editing requires far more creativity. If you don't have the right piece, you have to go out and shoot it, come back to the project, and add it in the proper place.

You view, arrange, rearrange, and enhance your clips in the Edit pane of the player window. When you first click this pane, you're given the option to use a blank template or an existing GoPro template for your project. For now, begin by using a blank template. See Chapter 10 for more about templates.

## Setting in and out points

To keep your audience interested in your movie, you need to show them the prime parts of each clip, so it's important to make sure that you remove the excess frames by setting in and out points. There's no sense in trying to convert a five-minute clip when all you need is 30 seconds of it for your movie.

Setting in and out points is also helpful in reducing the size of the converted file, and it eliminates any unwanted portions of the initial recording from being included in the converted file. It's like trimming the fat from your chicken cutlets, but you won't need to wash your hands when you're done.

GoPro Studio Edit offers a variety of ways to isolate the desired part of the clip:

- ✔ Set in and out points with a menu command. You can do this only on a Mac (see Chapter 10).
- ✔ Drag points on the playback slider (see Figure 11-6).
- ✔ Use the Split Clip tool. It looks like a razor blade and divides the section where you place the playhead.

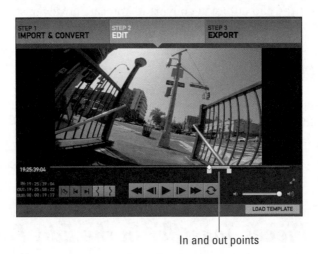

In and out points

Figure 11-6: In and out points on the playback slider.

Here's how to set in and out points:

1. **Select the clip in the Import Bin.**

2. **Move the playhead on the playback slider to the desired start point of the clip, and click the Mark In button to cut everything before that point.**

3. **Move the playhead on the playback slider to the desired end point of the clip, and click the Mark Out button to cut everything after that point.**

4. **Find other cuts on the same clip.**

    After you click the Add Clip to Conversion List button, you can grab other sections from the original clip by resetting the in and out points and clicking the Add Clip to Conversion List button. This adds it to the

Conversion List bin. This comes in handy when you have a long continuous clip with different elements you want for your movie.

5. **Repeat Steps 1–4 to set more in and out points.**

### Dragging clips to the Storyboard

After importing your clips, setting in and out points, and converting to the CineForm codec, you can drag them from the Import Bin to the Storyboard. The clips play in order from left to right, so be sure you drag them to the proper place.

# Assembling Clips in the Storyboard

After gathering your clips, and setting the in and out points, it's time to arrange them on the Storyboard. Located below the player window, this is the place where you decide the order the clips play, thus combining multiple clips into a single video. The Storyboard consists of one video track, two audio tracks, and two title tracks (see Figure 11-7).

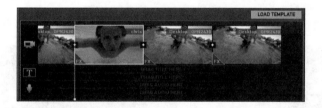

**Figure 11-7:** Storyboard shows video thumbnails and space for audio and title tracks.

Populating the Storyboard is as simple as dragging clips from the Media Bin (which occupies the same place as the Import Bin when you're in the Edit pane) into the Storyboard. Although you can drag clips around to change their order, it's more efficient to build the movie in sequential order when the clips are in the Storyboard. You can always modify the order of clips later.

Save your work often. It may seem to be excessive, but every time you make a change or add some interesting element, you should save the project.

### Adding clips

Here's how to add a clip to the Storyboard:

1. **Find the desired clip in the Media Bin.**

2. **Drag it to the Storyboard.**

As you drag, a green vertical line indicates the spot where the clip will be inserted.

3. **Release the mouse button to drop the clip.**

4. **Repeat Steps 1–3 to add more clips.**

5. **Save the project by choosing File➪Save.**

Clips use the same thumbnail in the Media Bin and the Storyboard, but clip information changes slightly in the Storyboard.

A yellow border around the thumbnail indicates a selected clip (refer to Figure 11-7). Other information includes

- ✔ **Filename:** The filename is based on how you set preferences, mentioned in Chapter 10.

- ✔ **Delete a clip:** Poof! It's gone. By dragging this triangle on the lower left of the thumbnail off the top, as seen in Figure 11-8, you remove all applied effects such as color, framing, and exposure.

- ✔ **Mute button:** Click this button to toggle audio for the selected clip.

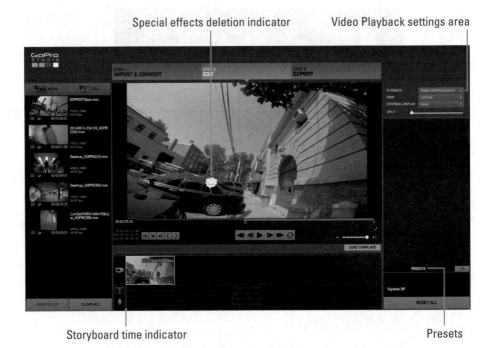

Figure 11-8: Deleting special effects.

## Cropping images

The Framing controls, found in the Video Playback settings, allow you to change the composition of your clips. This feature comes in handy when you want to isolate a portion of the scene or crop a distracting element. Depending on the amount of area you crop, you may lose some detail. If you shot the footage in 4K, however, you can crop a good portion of the image and still have more than enough resolution when saving the file in HD.

Just select the clip you want to alter on the Storyboard, go to the Video Playback settings area, and then click the down arrow next to Framing to display the Framing controls (see Figure 11-9).

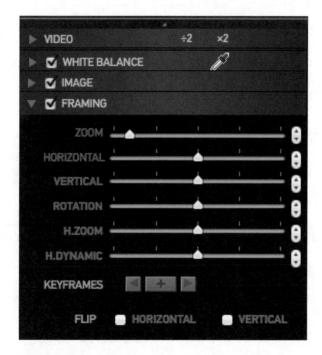

Figure 11-9: The Framing controls allow you to adjust and position an image to your liking.

Here's what each Framing control does:

- **Zoom:** Use this slider to make the image larger or smaller.

- **Horizontal:** Use this slider to move the image left or right. This feature works best with a cropped image so that the frame remains filled. An uncropped image shows black at either end.

✓ **Vertical:** Use this slider to move the image up or down. This feature works best with a cropped image so that the frame remains filled. An uncropped image shows black at the top or bottom.

✓ **Rotation:** Use this slider to rotate the clip. A cropped image maintains a full frame.

✓ **H.Zoom:** When you're mixing 4x3 and 16x9 video sources, use this slider to adjust the horizontal scaling of the image. 4x3 looks like the aspect ratio of your old television set; 16x9 resembles the current wide screen.

✓ **H.Dynamic:** Use this slider to adjust the horizontal stretch point of the image. This control, which is best used in tandem with the H.Zoom control, helps preserve the normal appearance of people who have been stretched by 4x3-to-16x9 conversion.

✓ **Keyframes:** These controls allow you to create different frame sizes in the same clip so you can zoom, pan, and rotate while the clip is playing.

✓ **Flip:** Select the Horizontal or Vertical check box to enable horizontal or vertical flipping of the image. Select both of these options if you shot your scene upside-down and want to correct it.

## Splitting clips

Sometimes, you want to split a large clip and insert a new clip between its parts. Splitting a clip is as easy as cutting a piece of pie. Just follow these steps:

1. **Select the clip you want to split.**

   Move the playhead or the Storyboard time indicator (depending if you're working from the player or Storyboard, respectively) to the location where you want to insert the new clip.

2. **Click the Split button to split the clip.**

   If you position the playhead on the first frame of a clip, clicking the Split button cuts the clip in half.

3. **Drag a new clip between the two split clips.**

## Fine-tuning clips

You can fine-tune clips in several ways:

✓ **Rearrange clips.** To rearrange the order of clips, drag them in the storyboard. A green line appears as you drag a clip, indicating a new location for the clip.

✓ **Delete a clip.** Select it on the Storyboard and drag it up and get it a poof! The little cloud that lets you know it disappeared (refer to Figure 11-8). Or just select it and press the Delete key.

✓ **Trim a clip.** When you're fine-tuning your edit, you may want to shave a few seconds off a clip to make the movie smoother. Just reset the in and out points (refer to "Setting in and out points" earlier in this chapter), and you're good to go.

## Adjusting white balance

The White Balance controls let you alter the color of the scene to either correct or enhance the way you remembered the scene. Although GoPro captures color fairly accurately, sometimes you need to enhance the scene, and this feature does the trick. Just click the little triangle next to the White Balance choice on the right side of the window. The feature consists of a couple sliders, an eyedropper, and keyframe adjustments. Click the movie clip you want to enhance in the Storyboard, and make your adjustments.

You can changes the color doing one of the following:

✓ **Temperature slider:** Move the slider to adjust the color temperature of the clip, ranging from cool to warm. You can also adjust temperature using the step controls just to the right of the slider.

✓ **Tint slider:** Move the slider to adjust the tint, ranging from cool to warm. You can also adjust tint using the step controls just to the right of the slider.

✓ **Eye Dropper:** When you use the eyedropper to click on something white (or something that's supposed to be white) in the frame, it adjusts the overall color. So if the area you click on was a little blue, the correction will neutralize the blue and warm up the image.

✓ **Keyframes:** You can change color as the clip plays by setting keyframes at various points. Move the playhead to a desired area, and click the + button. Change the White Balance, or more appropriately, the color in the image. It will play until you set another keyframe and make another change. Every time you repeat this, it will change the tone at that point in the clip.

## Adjusting tones with the Image feature

You can make tonal adjustments to your movie clip to make it look just right. Just click the little triangle next to the Image choice on the right side of the window. The feature consists of several sliders and keyframe adjustments. Click the movie clip you want to enhance in the Storyboard, and make your adjustments.

Here's what the controls do:

- **Exposure:** Basically, it allows you to make the movie clip lighter or darker.
- **Contrast:** Adds or decreases image contrast.
- **Saturation:** Enhances color in the image, or can take it away. This is a cool effect for stylizing your movie.
- **Sharpness:** Adds, or takes away, sharpness in the image.
- **Keyframes:** You can make the color change to your specifications in a movie clip by setting keyframes at various points. Each time you set a keyframe, it makes a change to the color (in this case) from that point on (or until you set another keyframe). Move the playhead to a desired area, and click the + button. Make another tonal adjustment, and it will play until you set another keyframe and make another change. Every time you repeat this, it will change the tone at that point in the clip.

TECHNICAL STUFF

## Applying the "Ken Burns" effect

You can add motion to an otherwise-static video by using the *Ken Burns effect,* an effect named after the award-winning creator of such films as *The Civil War, Baseball,* and *Jazz.* Burns mastered the technique of making still photos appear to move onscreen by zooming, panning, and rotating them.

Here's how you can apply this effect:

1. **Select a clip in the Storyboard.**

2. **Display the Framing controls (refer to Figure 11-9).**

3. **Place the playhead on the part of the clip you want to change.**

4. **Click the + button to add a framing keyframe to the clip.**

5. **Make the desired changes.**

   Use the Zoom slider to make the clip larger, for example, or you can change any of the other settings.

6. **Repeat Steps 1–5 for all clips you want to change.**

7. **Save the project.**

A few tips won't hurt:

- **Pace the movement.** Never zoom in or out of a scene too quickly or too slowly.

- **Make sure that the movement has a purpose.** Don't make an image larger haphazardly; do it intentionally. Let the zoom or the pan show viewers what they should be looking at.

- **Pan properly.** A *pan* is a camera movement from left to right. If you pan video that you've already shot, you get a black area that gets larger as you move, as in the top figure below. Instead, crop the image so that you have enough image real estate to keep the frame full, as in the bottom figure below.

- **Crop the image.** If you rotate the image, be sure to crop it enough so you don't show the black on the edge or corners.

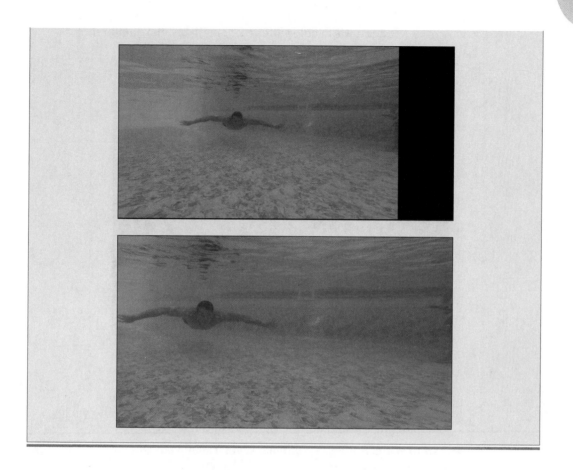

## Working with presets

GoPro Studio Edit lets you stylize your video with a series of preset effects, found on the bottom-right side of the window. Using these presets is quick and easy, and can help your movie make a statement. All you have to do is select a clip on the Storyboard and then click an effect. If you don't like it, click the Reset All button, on the bottom right, or click and drag the FX triangle on the clip to make it go away.

### Using existing presets

You can use the following presets:

✔ **None:** Restores all default settings.

✔ **Protune:** Makes a flat clip look punchier by increasing saturation and contrast. (For more on Protune, see Chapter 4.)

✔ **1970s:** Applies a warm color filter that simulates film shot in the '70s (see Figure 11-10).

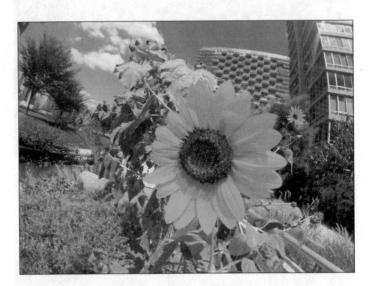

**Figure 11-10:** This sunflower picture takes on a retro look with the 1970s filter applied to it.

✔ **4X3 Center Crop:** Zooms in on a clip shot at a 4:3 aspect ratio while cropping the top and bottom portions of the image.

✔ **4X3 to Wide:** Applies a combination of framing adjustments to transform a clip shot in 4:3 aspect ratio to a 16:9 image.

✔ **Candy Color:** Applies a highly saturated color effect to the clip.

✔ **Day for Night:** Makes a scene shot during the day look as though it was shot at night (see Figure 11-11).

✔ **Hot Day:** Creates a warm color effect that simulates being close to the sun.

✔ **Night Vision:** Makes the video look as though it was shot through night-vision goggles by applying a green tint (see Figure 11-12).

✔ **Sepia:** Applies a brownish, unsaturated filter to create a sepia effect.

✔ **Vignette Large:** Blurs the edges of the frame, as in an old photograph.

✔ **Vignette Medium:** Provides a more subtle vignette effect.

✔ **Vignette Off:** Turns vignette off on the image.

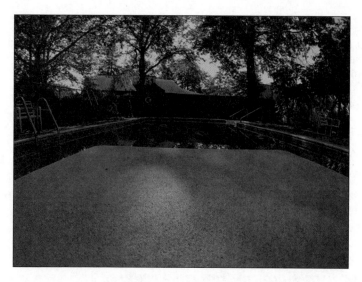

**Figure 11-11:** Shooting a night scene during the day is easier than shooting a day scene as night.

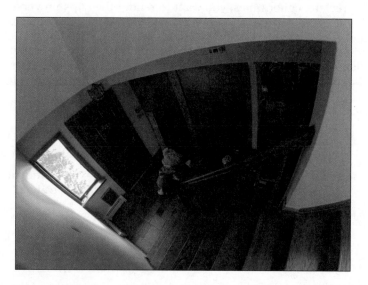

**Figure 11-12:** This cool effect makes your movie look like *The Blair Witch Project.*

### Making your own presets

On the off chance that you're not crazy about GoPro Studio Edit's presets (see the preceding section), you can make your own. The process is simple. Just follow these steps:

1. **Select a clip in the Storyboard.**

2. **Use the White Balance, Image, and Framing controls to create the look you want for the video.**

3. **Click the little gear icon next to Preset Title to open the Manage Presets window.**

4. **Click the + button, type a new preset name, and check the setting you want to save.**

5. **Click OK.**

## Adding slow motion and reverse

Sometimes there's nothing like slow motion for getting your point across, especially if you want to emphasize a situation that normally plays out too fast. Maybe you performed a jump on a BMX bike and it plays too fast to appreciate. Other times, you want to render the clip in reverse to capture a world gone backwards. A great example is a clip of someone jumping out of the water and onto the diving board. Whatever you choose, GoPro Studio Edit makes it easy to accomplish. Just click on the little triangle next to the Video choice on the right side of the window. The feature consists of a couple sliders that control speed and fade. There's also a check box for reverse.

Here's what the controls do:

- ✔ **Speed:** Adjusts the duration of the clip from 1 percent to 1,000 percent. That allows you to slow down the clip, as well as speed it up.

- ✔ **Fade In:** Fades the clip from black. You can choose the duration using the slider or text entry box on the right side of the slider.

- ✔ **Fade Out:** Fades the clip to black.

## Managing Audio Matters

GoPro Studio Edit uses Storyboard editing as opposed to a timeline, so editing a movie is a matter of assembling trimmed clips to play in order. The program offers some flexibility when it comes to audio, adding up to two additional tracks for sound effects, background music, or voiceovers.

When using a GoPro edit template, the soundtrack uses one of the tracks, so you're left with only one.

Because audio plays such a big part in a movie, it's important to treat it with some TLC, fine-tuning the levels of your clips, laying down the right music for the soundtrack, and maybe adding a voiceover.

GoPro Studio Edit currently supports the following audio formats: MP3, M4A, WAV, and AIFF.

## Adding an audio track

Nothing gives your footage a real movie feel like adding a soundtrack, and GoPro Studio Edit makes that easy to do. You can also include a voiceover. The only limitation is that you can add only two tracks.

Audio is like video, in that you must import it into GoPro Studio Edit. Follow these steps:

1. **Click the Add Media button at the top of the Media Bin.**

2. **In the resulting dialog box, browse to your audio file, select it, and click Open.**

   A thumbnail of a microphone on a music staff appears in the bin.

3. **Drag the file to the Storyboard.**

   As you drag, a green box indicates the spot where the file will be inserted, making it easier for you to line up the audio file with other portions of your Storyboard.

   Dragging an audio file on top of an existing video clip causes the audio file to start at the same time as that video clip.

4. **Revise the file if necessary.**

   After placing an audio file, you can rearrange it by dragging it to a new location. You can also change its duration by dragging its edges.

## Correcting an audio track

Because you capture audio under a variety of circumstances, sometimes audio levels are inconsistent. GoPro Studio Edit makes problems easy to fix. The Audio Setting features include a few controls for adjusting audio levels and fading sound in and out.

- ✔ **Level dB:** Allows you to change the volume level of the clip during playback. You can increase the level for soft clips and decrease it for loud or distorted clips.

- ✔ **Fade In:** Gradually raises the audio level from silence.

- ✔ **Fade Out:** Gradually lowers the audio level to silence.

# Working with Titles

Great video, clear audio, nice layout, and a rocking soundtrack . . . check, check, check, and check. You need just one more thing to make a great movie: a title. You can use two tracks for titles, which can be superimposed over clips or appear directly above them on the Storyboard.

## Adding a title

To add a title to your movie, follow these steps:

1. **Click the Add Title button at the top of the Media Bin in the Edit Pane.**

   A title thumbnail appears in the Media Bin.

2. **Drag the thumbnail to a title track in the Storyboard.**

   As you drag, a green box indicates the spot where the title will be inserted, which makes it easier for you to line up the title with other portions of your Storyboard.

3. **Double-click the thumbnail.**

   A dialog box appears on the right side of the project window.

4. **Type the title.**

5. **Adjust the font, size, and other details (see Figure 11-13).**

## Adjusting a title

There's an art to using titles, part of which revolves around duration.

A rule of thumb is that a title should stay onscreen long enough for viewers to be able to read it twice.

To adjust the duration of a title, follow these steps:

1. **Select the title on the Storyboard.**

   A title has a yellow box surrounding it.

2. **Drag the edges of the yellow box to change the title's duration.**

   Alternatively, set a new out point for the title by clicking the Mark Out button or moving the out point marker on the playback slider (refer to Figure 11-8).

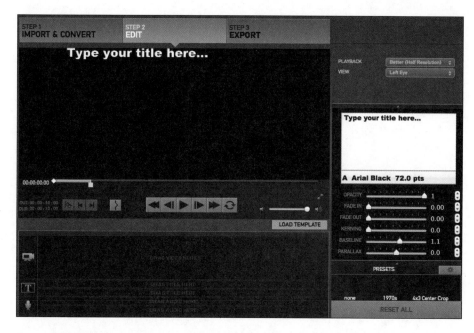

**Figure 11-13:** Making titles takes a few keystrokes and enhances your movie.

## Changing title properties

This panel, found on the left side on the window, provides several controls that you can use to change various attributes of a title:

- ✔ **Opacity:** Changes the transparency of the text.
- ✔ **Baseline:** Adjusts the spacing between lines when a title has multiple lines of text.
- ✔ **Kerning:** Adjusts spacing between letters.
- ✔ **Parallax:** Adjusts the position of the text in 3D space.
- ✔ **Fade In:** Changes the title's in point.
- ✔ **Fade Out:** Changes the title's out point.

12

# Presenting Your Movie

### In This Chapter

- Converting files for export
- Exporting your movie
- Sharing the movie
- Choosing long-term storage

Whether your movie consists of a few clips from the GoPro you mounted on a lawn mower, an elaborate edit of your backyard-pool Olympics, or a short movie of your dramatic friends, it's time to kick it out of GoPro Studio Edit and get it out into the world.

Will you upload it to a video-sharing website? Send it out as a live stream? Go old-school and burn it to a Blu-ray DVD? You have many possibilities to consider.

Maybe you're not even looking to make an exclusively GoPro movie; instead, you want to incorporate some GoPro footage into a bigger movie project. That's no problem, because the process of using the program, and ultimately exporting your edit, remains the same.

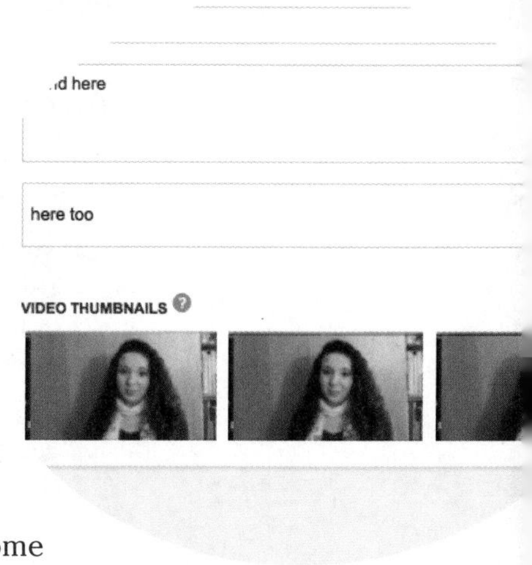
here too
VIDEO THUMBNAILS

After that, it's a matter of showing it to the world.

## Converting Your Movie Files for Export

Although GoPro Studio Edit (see Chapter 11) provides some options for exporting your movie, it offers limited choices. Although many may work for your needs, you can export your movie from GoPro Studio Edit and use a conversion program to create a file that meets your specific needs.

Conversion programs do more than make video files viewable in another file format: They also allow you to customize resolution, quality settings, audio settings, bit rate, and other settings. Convert your uncompressed file to an MP4 file, for example, or transform an AVI file to an FLV file for embedding in a web page. Whatever you choose to do, the software does the work.

### MPEG Streamclip

If you're looking to convert your movie to another format with lots of options and don't feel like spending a lot of money, check out MPEG Streamclip. It's powerful, it's free, and it handles multiple formats and sizes. It also is available for both Macintosh and Windows.

Because it's designed exclusively for exporting and encoding files in a variety of formats, MPEG Streamclip gets the job done quickly. It supports the following formats:

| | | |
|------|------|--------|
| AC3  | M2P  | MPA    |
| AVI  | M2T  | MPEG   |
| AVR  | M2V  | MPV    |
| AIFF | MMV  | PS REC |
| DAT  | MOD  | TS VID |
| DV   | MOV  | VOB    |
| M1A  | MP2  | VRO    |
| M1V  | MP4  |        |

You can download it at www.squared5.com.

### Other conversion programs

If you need a little more horsepower for converting your files, here are a couple of reasonably priced programs.

- **AVS Video Converter (Windows only):** This program handles an extensive list of video file types (including Blu-ray) and provides a wide array of tools and effects. At this writing, the software costs $59. You can download a trial version at www.avs4you.com.

- **Xilisoft Video Converter Ultimate (Windows and Macintosh):** This conversion program handles most file types and supports a variety of mobile devices, music players, and gaming platforms. At this writing, the program costs $50. You can download a trial version at www.xilisoft.com.

## Getting That Movie Out There

When you've put your movie together, applied every possible effect that GoPro Studio Edit has to offer, performed any necessary conversions (see the preceding section), and saved it, you're ready to export it.

After you export a movie, you no longer need software to play it, because the file becomes self-playing. You can watch it on any computer, mobile device, and even your big screen television.

## Choosing export options

Sometimes, you have a definitive plan for the movie, so it's simple to pick the export settings you need for it. At other times, the process is a little more complicated. You may have used a low-quality setting, only to find out that what looks pretty good on a smartphone looks pretty bad on a video-sharing website and atrocious on a big-screen television set. To make the right choices about everything from resolution to playback bit rate, you need to have informed opinions.

You have two ways to export and share: You can export your movie, either by clicking the tab of the Export work area, or by using the pull-down menu. On a Mac, go to Share➪Export Movie. You'll see the choices for sharing, as shown in Figure 12-1. On a PC, go to File➪Export movie.

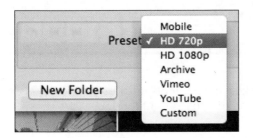

Figure 12-1: The Export dialog with the pull-down menu on a Mac.

GoPro Studio Edit provides many ways to export your files. Following are the program's export options:

- ✔ **Mobile:** Sizes your video appropriately for viewing on smartphones and other mobile devices.

- ✔ **HD 720p:** Exports a high-definition (HD) movie file.

- ✔ **HD 1080p:** Exports a full HD movie.

- ✔ **Archive:** Exports the file with the CineForm codec.

- ✔ **Vimeo:** Exports the file in full HD for sharing on the Vimeo website.

- ✔ **YouTube:** Exports the file in resolutions up to full HD for sharing on YouTube.

- ✔ **Custom:** Lets you create your own versions of some of the preceding options.

> # Video settings defined
>
> Here are some of the video settings you'll use when exporting video:
>
> ✓ **Bit rate:** By definition it refers to the number of bits displayed over a period of time, usually one second. But you will know it as a number that provides the most video quality the higher it goes. The problem is that as bit rate climbs, so does the file size, hence the reason there are so many for you to choose.
>
> ✓ **H264:** One of the most common video compression formats, it saves the video file in a smaller file with very little loss of quality.
>
> ✓ **CineForm:** The native file format for working with GoPro files.
>
> ✓ **Source Frame Rate:** The frames per second the video was captured in.
>
> ✓ **Exported Frame Rate:** Regardless of how many frames per second you captured the footage in, GoPro Studio Edit will export most files at 29.97 frames per second, but depending on the preset, you can get 59.94 frames per second.
>
> ✓ **Resolution:** It's the number of pixels that you captured the movie file in. If you captured in HD, it would have a resolution of 1920x1080. 4K video is double that, while NTSC covers 720x480.

The following sections take a deeper look at GoPro Studio Edit's export options to help you find the one that's right for you.

### Mobile

This option is the perfect choice for exporting a movie that you want to play smoothly on a mobile phone — the kind of thing you want to send via email or show as a work in progress. You never want this version of a file to be the only export of a movie unless you don't really care about it. Here are the settings:

✓ **Resolution:** No matter what resolution you used to shoot the movie, this setting changes it to 640x360p (pixels).

✓ **Compression:** This setting applies the H.264 compression format.

✓ **Bit Rate:** This setting is 1.5MB per second — a very low rate, so both video and audio quality will suffer. But because the file is intended to be viewed only on a mobile phone, the quality will suffice.

✓ **Exported Frame Rate:** The file will have a maximum frame rate of 29.97 frames per second (fps).

### HD 720p

This option creates a smaller HD file that provides the perfect compromise between quality and file size. Think of it as HD light — something that plays online with excellent quality. Here are the settings:

✔ **Resolution:** No matter what resolution you used to shoot the movie, this setting changes it to 1280x720p.

✔ **Compression:** This setting applies the H.264 compression format.

✔ **Bit Rate:** This setting varies with the frame rate at which you captured the footage. Footage captured at a frame rate higher than 29.97 fps gets a healthy bit rate of 15MB per second; anything with a lower frame rate lower has a bit rate of 7MB per second.

✔ **Exported Frame Rate:** This setting varies based on native resolution but goes no higher than 59.94 fps.

### HD 1080p

This option is the default for export and provides the greatest quality. It's perfect for playing your movie on a big screen or burning it to DVD. If you want to upload your movie to a video-sharing site or send it to a friend to watch on a smartphone, however, it's a bit much. Here are the settings:

✔ **Resolution:** No matter what resolution you used to shoot the movie, this setting changes it to 1920x1080p.

✔ **Compression:** This setting applies the H.264 compression format.

✔ **Bit Rate:** This setting produces an optimum-quality bit rate of 15MB per second, which creates a great experience for the viewer as well as an enormous file.

✔ **Exported Frame Rate:** This setting varies based on native resolution but goes no higher than 59.94 fps.

### Archive

This export option retains the program's original codec by creating a CineForm file with a user-selectable quality level. This option is your best choice if you want to export a high-quality master file for broadcast or archival purposes. Here are the settings:

✔ **Resolution:** This setting preserves the resolution at which you shot the movie.

✔ **Compression:** This setting applies the CineForm codec. On a Windows PC, you can choose a CineForm AVI or MOV format.

✔ **Bit Rate:** This setting doesn't apply a numerical bit rate; it allows you to choose Low, Medium, or High.

✔ **Exported Frame Rate:** This setting applies the native frame rate of each clip.

### Vimeo

Choose this option for movies that you want to export to the Vimeo video-sharing site. Here are the settings:

- ✔ **Resolution:** This setting applies native resolution up to 1080p. Files with resolution higher than 1080p are center-cropped and scaled to 1080p.
- ✔ **Compression:** This setting applies the H.264 compression format.
- ✔ **Bit Rate:** This setting varies with resolution, applying a bit rate of 15MB per second to files with resolution of 1080p or higher. For clips with resolution below 1080p, the setting applies a lower bit rate of 7MB per second.
- ✔ **Exported Frame Rate:** This setting is native to the frame rate of each clip but never higher than 29.97 fps.

### YouTube

Choose this option for movies that you want to export to the YouTube video-sharing site. Here are the settings:

- ✔ **Resolution:** This setting applies native resolution up to 1080p. Files with resolution higher than 1080p are center-cropped and scaled to 1080p.
- ✔ **Compression:** This setting applies the H.264 compression format.
- ✔ **Bit Rate:** This setting varies with resolution, applying bit rate of 8MB per second for files with resolution of 1080p files or higher. For clips with resolution below 1080p, the setting applies a lower bit rate of 5MB per second.
- ✔ **Exported Frame Rate:** This setting applies the native frame rate of each clip and supports rates of up to 59.94 fps.

### Custom

If you don't find the other export settings to be to your liking, you can build your own, choosing the format, frame size, frame rate, and quality settings. The Custom dialog (see Figure 12-2) allows you to customize your movie for export as follows:

- ✔ **Resolution:** You can select a resolution up to 1920x1080p.
- ✔ **Compression:** Choose H.264 or CineForm compression.
- ✔ **Bit Rate:** Use a slider to set a bit rate of 1MB to 50MB per second. CineForm uses a slider between low and high.
- ✔ **Exported Frame Rate:** This setting applies the native frame rate of each clip and supports rates of up to 59.94 fps.

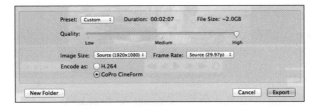

Figure 12-2: Custom dialog options.

## *Exporting your movie on a Mac*

The Export pane of the player window is where you export your movie in the desired format and with the desired settings.

Exporting is quite simple. Follow these steps:

1. **Choose Share⇨Export Movie or click the Export pane.**

   The dialog shown in Figure 12-3 appears.

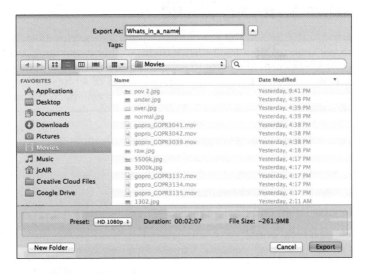

Figure 12-3: The Export dialog.

2. **Type a name for your file in the Export As text box.**

3. **Choose a preset from the Presets drop-down menu.**

4. **Click Export.**

   Within a few moments, a self-playing movie is ready.

### *Exporting your movie in Windows*

Because the Mac and Windows version of GoPro Studio Edit differ somewhat, the process is slightly different when exporting your movie.

1. **Click Export or choose File⇨Export.**

2. **Type a name for your file in the Export As text box.**

3. **Choose your preset.**

   On the bottom right of the dialog, you find the Presets drop-down menu.

4. **Click Export.**

   Within a few moments (or many, depending on the file size), a self-playing movie is ready.

After you export your movie file, be sure to watch it for quality control. Make sure that the file format and size you applied look as good as possible. If you don't like it, trash it and export another copy that meets your approval.

## Sharing and Sharing Alike

Sharing movie files in the era of the hit television series *Mad Men* was very different than we do it today. Back then, would-be moviemakers made copies of their silent 8mm film reels to send to family, friends, and film competitions. That spirit remains alive today, except instead of a physical movie, you're sending a virtual one. It's also not going to just one person, but many — maybe even millions.

Here are some of the ways you can share your movie:

- Upload it to video-sharing sites.
- Share it on social media.
- Share it on mobile devices.
- Send it via email.
- Burn it to DVD.

Movie files are big, and HD makes them bigger, so it's important to strike the right blend between file size and quality. Ideally, you compressed yours enough to upload on the Internet. Although each video-sharing site has different specifications, it's possible to upload a HD movie that's properly encoded.

## *Sharing your movie on Facebook*

The world's largest social media site, with around 1 billion active users, provides a great forum for your video. How many people actually see your video, of course, depends in part on the size of your Friends list and how many of your friends can get other people to check out the movie. Facebook allows you to upload a video directly from your computer, or you can post a link to YouTube if your video is posted there.

Be sure that you're using a recent web browser and have Adobe Flash loaded. Adobe Flash is necessary for the movie to play. If you don't have it, chances are you will be prompted to download it. If you already have it, then expect to be asked to update Flash periodically. Your movie should meet the following requirements:

- The video is no larger than 1,024MB.
- The video's length doesn't exceed 20 minutes.
- The video is an MP4 movie file using H.264 compression and the AAC audio format.
- You made the video yourself or have permission to share it.

Uploading a video to Facebook is relatively easy. Follow these steps:

1. **Navigate to the Facebook home page (`www.facebook.com`).**

   Make sure you have a Facebook account. If not, create one.

2. **Click the Add Photos/Video link at the top of the page (see Figure 12-4).**

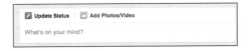

Figure 12-4: The Add Photos/Video link.

3. **Click the Add Video pane (see Figure 12-5), click Choose File, and navigate to the desired file.**

Figure 12-5: The Add Video pane.

**4. Add a description of the movie, if you want (see Figure 12-6).**

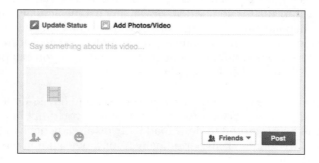

Figure 12-6: What you type here is what viewers will see.

**5. Click Post, and grab a cup of coffee.**

**6. Share the movie.**

Determine who gets to see it. You can share your movie with anyone on Facebook who can find it, your friends, or a group of your friends. Or just yourself.

## Sharing your movie on YouTube

YouTube records more than 3 billion video views per day, so your movie has the potential to be viewed by a lot of people — if they know it's available. If you're a little shy about reaching an audience, you can make your movies private and send would-be viewers an invitation to see it. The website supports a variety of file formats and allows some videos to be uploaded in full HD.

Here are a couple of YouTube requirements:

- Video length can't exceed 15 minutes unless you verify your account.
- You made the video yourself or have permission to share it.

Uploading a video to YouTube is relatively easy. Follow these steps:

**1. Navigate to the YouTube home page (www.youtube.com).**

**2. Sign in.**

Enter your username and password, or your Google login, as shown in Figure 12-7.

**3. Click Upload at the top of the page.**

After the upload screen, search for the video you want to share.

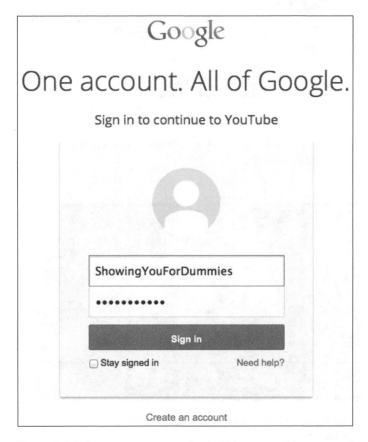

Figure 12-7: When you attempt to upload a video, you will be prompted to sign in.

**4. Select the video you want to upload.**

**5. Add details about the video while it's uploading.**

Depending on file size, uploading can take an hour or more. Use this time to name the movie and provide the proper information (see Figure 12-8).

**6. View your movie.**

Also keep an eye on the page views (see Figure 12-9) to see whether you'll have a viral favorite on your hands.

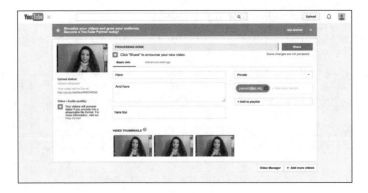

**Figure 12-8:** The more information you add here, the easier it is for your movie to find an audience.

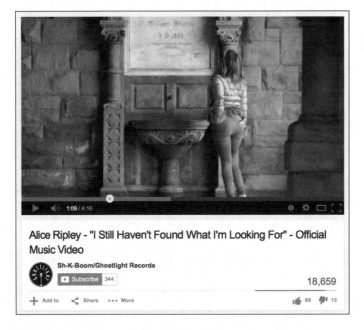

**Figure 12-9:** You can see how many people have viewed your video every time you look at it.

## Sharing your movie on Vimeo

Vimeo (an anagram for *movie*) is an alternative to YouTube. Because it supports higher quality, it's a popular place for independent filmmakers to upload, share, and view movies. Another notable difference from YouTube is that all uploaded content must be original and noncommercial.

Vimeo is a much smaller community than YouTube: The site has 8 million registered users and attracts around 65 million unique visitors per month.

Vimeo provides several levels of access: While free to upload video, users are limited to 500MB. An inexpensive Vimeo Plus account allows users a greater weekly upload amount, as well the capability to limit advertisements before the video, unlimited HD videos, and unlimited creation of channels, groups, and albums. Vimeo PRO provides the highest level of service and offers large storage, third-party video player support, and advanced analytics.

Uploading a video to Vimeo is simple. Follow these steps:

1. **Navigate to the Vimeo login page (`https://vimeo.com`).**

2. **Log in, using your Vimeo or Facebook login details.**

3. **Click the Upload a Video button.**

   The message shown in Figure 12-10 appears.

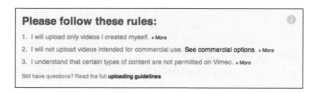

**Figure 12-10:** Vimeo takes content permissions seriously, so heed the warning before posting.

4. **Select the video you want to upload, and click the Upload Selected Videos button.**

   Depending on file size, uploading can take an hour or more.

5. **Name the movie and provide the proper description.**

6. **View your work.**

   You'll notice the sleeker presentation, as seen in Figure 12-11.

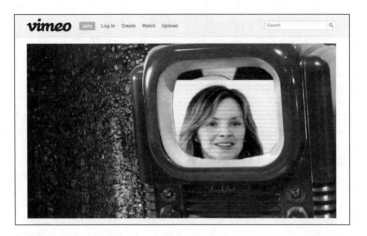

Figure 12-11: The Vimeo player occupies a fair amount of screen real estate.

# Finding the Best Archiving Solution

There's a great deal of uncertainty about the best way to save digital media files. Technology changes rapidly and is unstable at times. The problem of finding a stable solution is further compounded by imperfections in most of the storage methods at your disposal. This section presents some of the options.

## Choosing a file format

The first step in saving your beloved files is choosing the right file format. Here are a few options:

- **MOV:** Apple created this file format for use in its QuickTime program. It's a versatile format that allows you to save files in both compressed and uncompressed form. Use it when you want a self-playing file that you can also edit in another program without a loss of quality. It's ideal for broadcast.

- **MP4:** Also created by Apple, this format lets you compress files securely and (depending on the level of compression) with little loss in quality. This format uses the H.264 codec. These files can play back on iOS devices. This format is a perfect blend of quality and size, and can be delivered via email and FTP for broadcast playback.

- **AVI:** Microsoft's AVI (Audio Video Interweave) format saves files with a variety of compression formats and in several sizes. It doesn't retain aspect-ratio information, however.

✔ **CineForm:** CineForm is GoPro's proprietary codec and the one used when you save an archive copy in GoPro Studio Edit. It supports 3D and has been used for many feature films.

## Archiving on an external hard drive

External hard drives get faster and cheaper all the time, so they continue to be viable options for backing up your GoPro movies. With HD files occupying about five times the space of standard-definition (SD) files, however, the 2GB drive that you thought could never fill begins gasping for air. HD costs more to save, because the minutes of video per dollar ratio (breaking down capacity with file size) hasn't quite caught up with hard drive capacity. Of course, after you fill it you can move on to the next one.

Also, external hard drives have been known to fail from time to time, and they sometimes corrupt data, stop spinning, or burn out. You should always save important files on various drives and keep your fingers crossed.

## Backing up to tape

You can back your files up to tape if you have a camcorder or HD recording deck that uses tape. Professional production houses also back up to tape.

The upside of tape is that your footage can be played back on a television set or computer. You can digitize it by playing it into the program while it's recording.

The downside of tape is that tape is being phased out. Fewer decks for playback will be available over time, so finding someone to digitize your tapes may be difficult.

## Using Sony XD-CAM

Sony has replaced the videotape with this removable optical disc system for its HD video cameras. The Professional Disc has a storage capacity similar to a Blu-ray disc.

The XD-CAM is becoming the media choice for many broadcasters for their ENG crews and news production thanks to its versatility when it comes to shooting footage, editing, and archiving. In fact, the company boasts that more than 200 reality and news programs are using the Sony optical disc format. Sony also says it's a great choice for creating a long-term archive of footage.

While recording decks cost in upwards of five figures, you can take your important files to a production house and transfer them onto a Professional

Disc for about a hundred bucks. It's pricey, but its stability protects your best footage. Card readers are also available in the $3,000 range.

## Using media cards

Using media cards to store files, at least temporarily, has some merit. The prices of the cards are plunging, their capacity is rising, and their access time is increasing. That means you can play back an HD movie with no glitches.

Here are a few tips on using media cards:

- **Save as storage.** The intention is not necessarily to play video directly from the card, just to save the video file. You load the card, drag the files on it, and then safely eject.

- **Use a fast card.** If you plan to play video directly the card, be sure to use a fast-enough card. If you're not sure which speed will work for you, see Chapter 3.

- **Stick with common formats.** These days, common formats are Compact Flash (CF), Secure Digital (SD), and Memory Stick.

- **Be ready to transfer.** Because technology changes so rapidly, consider saving your files on newer media from time to time to ward off the evils of dust interfering with transfer or problems with the firmware of the drive or reader.

- **Keep the cards safe.** If media cards get wet, dusty, or stepped on, their content is lost.

## Storing in the cloud

You no longer have to worry about local media storage when you save in the cloud. Media files are uploaded to large servers in a techno netherland.

Most cloud sites offer free basic plans and use secure servers. Not all free plans are easy to use, however, making it hard to upload or find your files. Also, if your files are too big or you need to add space, you're either out of luck or have to pay a subscription fee to upgrade.

Longevity is also a concern. Although some cloud services are full-fledged online businesses, others aren't as successful. Stay current on site activity, and be prepared to move your files at the first sign that the service is closing.

Following are a couple of credible cloud services:

- **Dropbox:** This file-hosting service makes it easy to send files from one computer and access them on another by using a common folder on the Desktop. You drop files or folders into the Dropbox folder and send invitations to people, allowing them to access your material via an email link. Dropbox offers 2GB of storage space for free.

✔ **Hightail:** This reliable FTP service (formerly known as YouSendit) allows you to save and share large files. The free version provides 2GB of storage. A professional plan that costs $15.99 per month provides unlimited storage.

---

## Protecting your intellectual property

With modern video technology, the good news is you can easily share the movie with millions of potential viewers. That's also the bad news. Because your content can reach so many people some of them may use it without permission.

Here are a few ways to protect your video:

✔ **Use a watermark.** Sometimes a watermark is distracting, but it may deter content thieves by confirming that the content is yours.

✔ **Add a bug.** If you don't want to watermark your video, add a *bug* — a large icon in one corner of every frame. (You've probably seen bugs in programs on many television networks, such as ESPN.) Don't worry that the bug will affect sales or other legitimate use. Serious parties will ask you to send them a "clean" version.

✔ **Share cautiously.** Don't upload your video to just any place that will accept it. Instead, limit the number of sites to which you send movies, and keep a log of where and when you sent movies.

✔ **Search the web periodically for your movie.** Video pirates may be brazen but not always bright. You'd be surprised by how many users grab someone else's content and repost it under the original filename.

# Part IV
# The Part of Tens

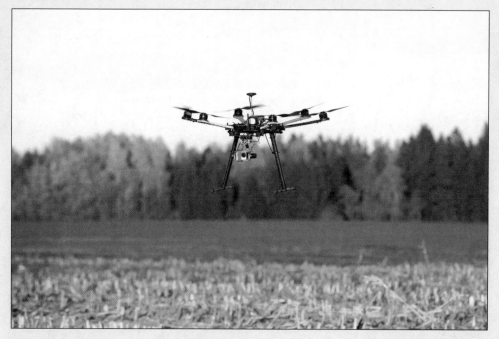

©istockphoto.com/intst Image #29397558

 Find out what to do with your GoPro professionally and for fun at
www.dummies.com/extras/goprocameras.

# In this part . . .

- Use your GoPro in fun ways.
- Find out how professionals use the GoPro camera.

# Ten Fun Ways to Use Your GoPro

*T*he GoPro brings out your fun side faster than a New York Jets jersey gets your green eyes to pop, provided that you have green eyes. Anyway, this little wonder lets you take a fresh perspective on the world. You can put it anywhere your heart desires and get some pretty cool stuff. This petite wonder has changed sports and adventure video, because it lets you capture scenes in places where cameras weren't always welcome.

In this chapter, you discover a fresh perspective to your moviemaking, including putting the camera in places that were never "camera-friendly," like in the water or up in the air. You can even attach it to your dog, or goat if you want, and see the world from his point of view. The sky is the limit when finding fun places for your GoPro.

## Make the Coolest Selfie

The selfie is quickly becoming one of the most prominent ways to take a portrait. Thanks to the wide-angle view of your GoPro, the camera lets you create some really interesting moving or still selfies.

Here are a few pointers for getting the best results:

✔ **Make the shot flattering.** More appropriately, keep it from becoming unflattering. The GoPro's wide-angle lens can distort your appearance, and holding it too low and close to your face can make your nose look like a weapon. Instead, hold it at just above eye level, perpendicular to the ground.

✔ **Know yourself.** What's your good side? If you know it, make sure that you shoot it.

✔ **Make sure that the light works.** Opt for soft directional light, as shown in Figure 13-1.

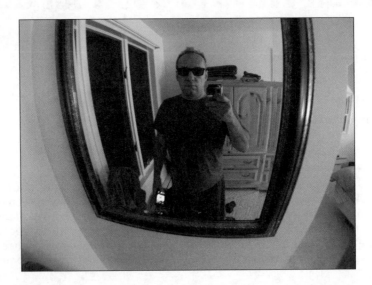

Figure 13-1: A GoPro selfie.

✔ **Mount the camera on an extension pole.** You can make a really fun shot by extending the camera at an angle above you or your group.

✔ **Be aware of the background.** Make sure that it's not too busy or too bright.

✔ **Use your smartphone as a monitor.** Here's something a little different: Hold the GoPro and keep your smartphone in view so that you have some idea how the shot will turn out.

## Explore Underwater

Maybe you're not an accomplished oceanographer, but you still desire to be the Jacques Cousteau of your local swimming hole. If so, the GoPro is ready, willing, and able to capture your views of the underwater world.

Here are some cool ways to take underwater photos and videos:

✔ **Swim with it.** Take the GoPro underwater, and mount it to your body or hold it as you navigate the deep. You can use it while snorkeling, scuba diving, or simply taking a dip in a pool (see Figure 13-2).

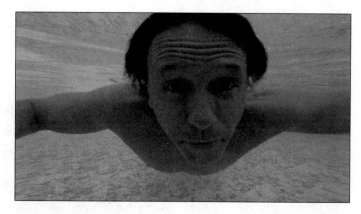

Figure 13-2: Swimming with a GoPro.

✔ **Use an extension pole underwater.** By attaching the camera to a pole and submerging it, you can get great underwater footage at a beach, pool, or lake.

✔ **Mount it underwater.** Use an existing mount, or jerry-rig your own; then put it in a pool or a shallow lake.

Just be careful that the GoPro doesn't get swept away or become a hazard to others.

✔ **Shoot at the surface.** Catch a rider on a boogie board, your mom on her raft, or the players in a water-polo match.

✔ **Monitor it with your smartphone.** Because most GoPro cameras don't include a viewfinder, and you don't want to get your smartphone wet, you can monitor the footage from the sidelines (in other words, away from the water).

# Walk through a Crowded Space

Capturing video of walking through a crowd isn't easy with a conventional camcorder. GoPro changes that situation, thanks to its small dimensions and wide view. You have lots of ways to move through a crowd with a GoPro attached to a headband or chest mount.

Here's how to use these mounts effectively:

- ✓ **Headband:** The GoPro is almost small enough that you can walk through a crowd with it unnoticed (see Figure 13-3).

  Try mounting the camera on your headband and looking behind you. This technique can provide some funny, compelling footage, especially when people get too close to you. You can monitor the scene by watching it on your smartphone.

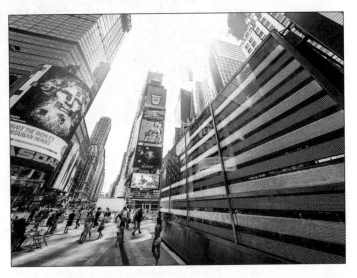

©istockphoto.com/FilippoBacci Image #46122936

**Figure 13-3:** Walking through Times Square provides an interesting perspective.

- ✓ **Chest harness:** Also known as the Chesty, this mount holds your GoPro at chest height, providing a slightly different perspective.
- ✓ **Wristband:** The wristband mount lets you grab shots to the side and shoot from the hip by holding the camera low and directly in your path. This technique helps you create some unique GoPro imagery.

## Attach It to Your Bike

Ambitious riders have long been mounting camcorders on their handlebars to record compelling video sequences. The GoPro can do the job too, with more options and from a unique perspective.

Consider the following possibilities:

- ✔ **Helmet mount:** This mount allows you to put the camera on your bicycle helmet. Wear the camera as you zip down bike paths or mountain trails, giving the viewer a truly authentic rider's-eye view.

  On the downside, the GoPro will capture motion from both the bike and the rider.

- ✔ **Handlebar mount:** This mount lowers the perspective and keeps the camera steady while providing the bike's point of view. Turn the camera around to get the rider's point of view.

- ✔ **Time-lapse video at night:** Point the camera at yourself and ride through a well-lit area, such as a busy downtown area at twilight.

## Take It Out on an ATV

If offroading is your thing, the GoPro can help you capture some great footage. Don't worry about the mud, sweat, and tears; the camera thrives under these conditions and handles them all with dignity.

Check out the following options for using your GoPro on an all-terrain vehicle (ATV):

- ✔ **Mount it on a roll bar.** GoPro makes a mount specifically for this point of view (see Figure 13-4).

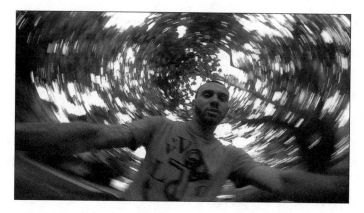

Figure 13-4: GoPro on a roll-bar mount.

- ✔ **Put it on the bumper.** This vantage point provides a rugged almost-ground-level view of the terrain, allowing the viewer to experience the excitement.

✔ **Mount it on a road course.** If you're traveling a specific road course, put a GoPro at a strategic location to get a unique perspective. (Just be careful that you don't run over it.)

✔ **Use multiple cameras.** Mount a camera inside the vehicle to show the driver; then mount other cameras on the roll bar, bumper, and even on the course to capture multiple points of view.

Wipe the lens after each take. There's nothing worse than having a great capture and finding goop on the lens.

## Shoot the View from the Sky

If you like flying remote-control planes as much as you like making cool videos, you'll love flying your GoPro on a quadcopter.

Here are a few cool ways to capture airborne video:

✔ **Fly it near fireworks.** Provided that you fly the quadcopter in safe areas (not over a large crowd or near a helicopter, for example), you can take an exciting new approach to filming a fireworks display.

✔ **Get an overhead shot of the beach.** Flying the GoPro over a beach can create interesting views of the sun and surf.

✔ **Capture your town from above.** It's pretty cool to look at a place you know well from an uncommon view. Capture everything from Main Street to your street for a fun and exciting video.

Abide by the rules. Always keep your quadcopter in your sight. Never fly it around another airborne vehicle or near an airport.

## Get a Dog's-Eye View

Provided that you have a big-enough dog, you can mount the camera on him to get the canine version of a bird's-eye view (see Figure 13-5). You have a few ways to mount the camera, with the best using the GoPro Fetch mount, which is designed specifically for your four-legged pal. Of course, fitting a small chest harness to the dog seems to work pretty well too. It may take a few adjustments to get the harness to fit snugly (and for the dog to get used to it, but that's nothing a few treats can't fix).

When the camera is mounted and on, just let your dog do his thing. The camera is lightweight, and if you mount it properly, it shouldn't cause the dog any discomfort.

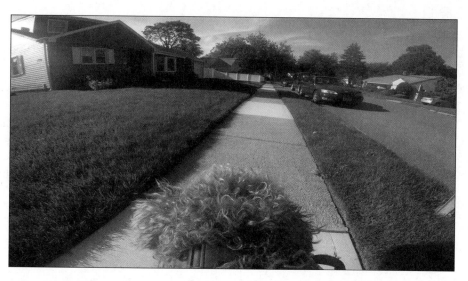

Figure 13-5: Dog's-eye view.

Try to shoot at a frame rate of 60 frames per second (fps) to compensate for the constant motion.

Here are some ideas:

- **Get a dog's view of the dog park.** Watching your dog interact with his canine buddies puts you right in the middle of the action.

- **Play fetch.** The time-honored game takes on new, exciting meaning when you see exactly what the dog sees.

- **Take your dog for a swim.** If your dog likes the water, the GoPro is ready for the challenge, providing some interesting footage.

When you're done with the shoot, have a treat ready!

## Make a Time-Lapse Movie

It's cool to shoot a bunch of still images to create a time-lapse movie. GoPro makes the process easy, with a special mode dedicated to time-lapse capture. You can speed up the world at the interval of your choosing for fun, or study changing scene over time. Shoot a sequence that shows a parade of commuters walking into the subway or fans filling a stadium, or record an expedited version of your child's Little League game. (Sometimes it's wishful thinking for a game to be that short.)

To make a time-lapse video, you need the following:

- ✔ **Proper settings:** Make sure that your GoPro is turned to Time-Lapse mode and set to the desired interval.

- ✔ **Sturdy mount:** Whichever mount you choose, make sure that it's sturdy and located away from excessive vibration.

- ✔ **Freshly charged battery:** The GoPro's battery doesn't last long, so when you're running the camera for an hour or so, you're at risk of a battery failure.

- ✔ **Something to help pass the time:** Although time-lapse recording produces an exciting effect, creating that recording isn't too exciting. Depending on how long you plan to capture frames, bring along a book and maybe a chair. Come to think of it, bring a beverage and a snack, too.

## Capture Your Own Band from the Stage

The GoPro provides an all-access pass to the center of any stage performance. Give the audience a perspective that only the band gets to see by using the removable instrument mount to capture footage right onstage.

Here are some of the places that a GoPro can go during a performance:

- ✔ **Guitar:** Mount the camera on the headstock, and position it to show the guitarist's fingers working the frets (see Figure 13-6). Put it on the guitar's body with a gooseneck mount to show the player picking. Turn the GoPro around to capture the rest of the band with your "guitar cam."

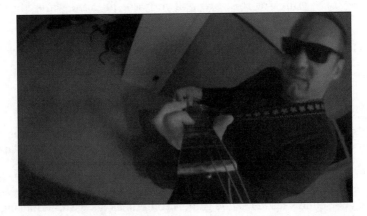

**Figure 13-6:** View of the frets from the neck down.

- ✔ **Drums:** As long as the drummer has enough space to drum, you can put the removable instrument mount anyplace. Use the gooseneck or jaws mount, depending on what you're trying to show.

- ✔ **Keyboards:** Put the camera above the keys to show a close-up and nicely distorted view of the keyboard player's hands.

- ✔ **Microphone stand:** Put the audience right in the middle of the action with a view from the microphone.

## Take GoPro in the Snow

The GoPro enables a new generation of family documentarians, extreme-sports aficionados, and ambitious filmmakers to cover winter sports and activities with relative ease and little worry about the equipment.

Here are some of the cool ways you can use your GoPro in the cold:

- ✔ **Ice skating:** Mount the camera to yourself, using one of the body mounts (headband, helmet, Chesty, and so on), and get a fresh view of a day at the rink.

- ✔ **Sledding:** Attach the GoPro to yourself or your sled to capture the sensation of flying down a snowy hill.

- ✔ **Skiing:** Mount the camera on yourself or use the pole mount to produce your own exciting ski video.

- ✔ **Snow tubing:** The helmet or headband mounts work great for this purpose, letting you capture the rush of going down the mountain. Shoot the scenery, or turn the camera around to record your buddy's expression.

- ✔ **Snowman time-lapse:** Mount the GoPro nearby and get to work on Frosty. Later, over hot chocolate, watch your hour-long effort in 45 seconds. Or mount the GoPro on a warm day to capture the hours-long melting process in less than a minute.

# Ten Professional Uses for GoPro Cameras

**D**o you make money shooting photos or video? By definition, you're a pro, no matter what your day job is. If you want to gain an edge, adding GoPro to your repertoire can help. Whether you shoot weddings, cover news stories, or create multimedia real estate listings, the GoPro can elevate the quality of the final product.

The camera is already gaining exposure on the pro circuit. Several reality television shows already incorporate GoPro cameras, including the CBS series *Survivor.*

This chapter presents ten professional uses for GoPro cameras.

## Wedding Videography

Depending on how ambitious the bride and groom want their nuptials video to be, the GoPro provides endless possibilities. Thanks to its portability, the camera stays out of the way to capture more natural activity. Most likely, you won't shoot the entire event with GoPro, but you can capture enough cool scenes to make things interesting.

Here are a few cool ideas:

- **Limo ride:** Mount one or more cameras in the car to document the transportation experience.

- **Dancing close-up:** Mount the GoPro on a pole or on your head, and get in close on the dance-floor action.

- **Table views:** Attach the GoPro to an extension pole, hold it above each table, and ask the guests to salute the bride and groom.

- **Low-angle portrait:** One cool trick is to lie on the ground with the camera facing upward, surrounded by the bridal party standing in a circular embrace. This technique works well for both still photos and videos.

# Real Estate Sales

Although it may not sound as exciting as capturing a surfer in a pipeline, there are many good reasons to use a GoPro to capture real estate interiors and exteriors, giving prospective buyers some informative images to consider.

Most pictures on real estate websites are ineffective images that don't represent the property accurately. Sometimes, they show too little of the property because they weren't shot with a wide-enough lens. Even with a moderately wide-angle lens, you can back up only so far before hitting a wall. The GoPro's lens is so wide that you may have the opposite problem, but it's certainly one you can work with.

Here are some ways to use the GoPro effectively in real estate:

- **Capture the entire room.** The camera's ultra-wide-angle lens lets you capture a whole room from some really tight spots (see Figure 14-1).

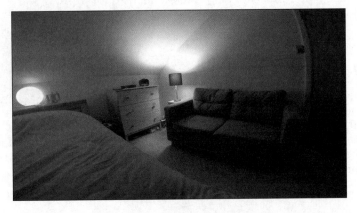

Figure 14-1: Capture the entire space without having to leave the room.

✔ **Do a walk-through.** When a prospective customer can't visit the property right away or just wants to vet it first, watching a video walk-through can be the next-best thing. Mounting the camera on a headband produces a perspective conducive to what your eyes see when walking through a crowded space.

✔ **Go aerial.** Mount a GoPro on a remote-control quadcopter, and fly it over the house to give the viewer a bird's-eye perspective of the property.

# Multimedia Reporting

Peek into any multimedia reporter's bag, and you're likely to find a variety of tools: a laptop computer, a smartphone loaded with apps, some sort of camcorder, and perhaps a GoPro camera.

Here are a few ways to use the GoPro on a reporting beat:

✔ **Record interviews.** You can capture the audio portion for radio highlights and also capture video to accompany the story online.

✔ **Capture raw footage.** It's best to capture a scene now and worry later about how you'll use it. Taking raw footage is better than not shooting at all and wishing that you had.

# Television News Production

The two roles may seem to be similar, but there's a dramatic difference between the functions of a multimedia reporter and a television producer. The latter relies solely on gathering visual images; the former uses various media to tell the story.

Most news crews use big cameras, but the portable GoPro provides a unique perspective. Even news cameras with expensive wide-angle lenses can't capture as wide a scene as a GoPro can. Also, you can mount a GoPro on a pole above the scene, which you can't do with a news camera; it's way too heavy (and expensive to replace if the pole breaks).

When you're covering television news, here are some ways that the GoPro can work for you:

✔ **Get a wide view of a news scene.** Parades, processions, red carpets, and other expansive events are easy to capture when you mount a GoPro nearby (see Figure 14-2).

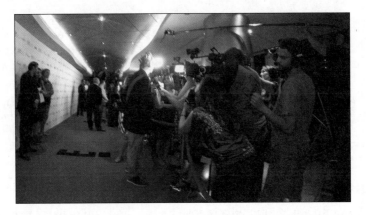

Figure 14-2: View from the red carpet provides a unique cutaway.

- ✒ **Film in tight spaces.** Sometimes, you need to capture news footage from a cramped space. Use a GoPro to fill the frame with all you need.

- ✒ **Create unique visual hooks.** The ultra-wide-angle lens creates footage that integrates nicely with conventional footage for both practical reasons (getting more into the scene) and aesthetic ones (getting a fish-eye view).

## Home Security

While not its main job, GoPro is perfect for keeping an eye on things. Sure, there are less expensive ways to observe a scene, but GoPro can come through in a pinch. Though it's small, it's not as small as a nannycam, you know, the ones hidden in a stuffed teddy bear. Although not as cute as those peeking bears, GoPro blows away the competition with its superior quality image. Because it's already designed for mounting, there's not the dilemma of "how am I gonna mount my camcorder outside my front door?" With GoPro, you can easily put in anywhere and start observing.

On the downside, the battery doesn't last that long and you have to control it from a nearby smartphone or remote. But it can still work.

Here are some ideas:

- ✒ **Mount it on a pole:** Observe the scene using your smartphone or device. You can control when to record and when to stop.

- ✒ **Put it in the baby's room:** If you don't have a video monitor, the GoPro provides a great solution.

✔ **Monitor an entrance or exit:** Whether you're watching the door and want to see who's coming and going, or just need to keep an eye on things. GoPro lets you temporarily place a camera anywhere to observe activity. Plus it's small enough to fit in cramped spaces.

## Traditional Sports Shooters

The GoPro works well for recording sports, whether they're high-school games or local sports events. Regardless of what you plan to use the camera for, capturing great action footage with it is easy.

Thanks to the camera's durability, coaches in many sports use it to record footage for future reference. Some Little League coaches, for example, use the GoPro as a teaching tool to help young players perfect their mechanics.

Here are a few ideas for recording a few popular sports:

✔ **Baseball:** Mount a GoPro on a catcher's mask to get a clear view of a pitch after release. Place a camera in the batting cage to capture footage for later evaluation by players and coaches. Wear a camera on a hat to capture a fielder's perspective.

✔ **Basketball:** Try mounting a GoPro (or two) on a glass backboard. You can shoot the full-court game on a conventional camcorder and edit in the backboard shots later, as appropriate.

✔ **Swimming:** Mount one or more GoPros in the pool to add an exciting aspect to swim-meet coverage. You can combine this footage with footage captured above the water on another camera.

✔ **Skiing:** Capture what a skier sees by putting a GoPro on a ski pole, using a pole mount. Or put the camera on a headband or helmet mount.

## Extreme Sports Shooters

Extreme sports make for exciting video. Following are some extreme sports that go well with the GoPro:

✔ **Surfing:** Photographers and filmmakers have mounted cameras on surfboards for years, but it did require an expensive waterproof housing and was a bit cumbersome on the board. GoPro is small and out of the way.

✔ **Skateboarding:** Use the skateboard mount to get a low-angle view (see Figure 14-3), or mount the camera on a skater's helmet to produce heartskipping skateboarding video.

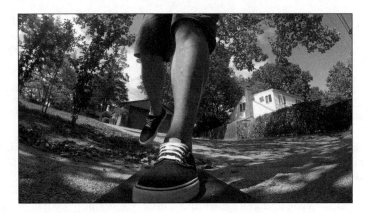

Figure 14-3: Skateboard view of an afternoon stroll.

✔ **Skydiving:** Mount the camera on a diver's helmet to capture the free fall and the parachute opening.

Because of the speeds involved in skydiving, it's a good idea to use a high frame rate — 60 frames per second (fps) or more.

## Independent Filmmaking

Anyone who ever made a film understands the extended time and high cost of shooting. The GoPro makes a positive difference. Because the camera is so cheap, you can put several of them all over a scene and not have to worry about making alternative takes.

You need to use the GoPro sparingly in filmmaking, however, due to its super-wide view. An actor who requests a close-up will think twice about asking for it again when the GoPro makes him look like a bobblehead doll.

## Documentary Filmmaking

You probably don't want to shoot the entire documentary with a GoPro. Instead, use it as a secondary camera, blending its footage with conventional footage. That way, you give yourself some cool choices for editing. These include:

✔ **Tight spaces:** So many times, it's not possible to get a wide enough view with your camcorder, so don't stress about it anymore; just mount a GoPro or two in the room for those situations.

✓ **Capture action:** That's what the camera is designed for, and that's how you should use it when shooting scenes for your documentary.

✓ **Point-of-view (POV):** A common practice with documentaries is to make the viewers feel like they're part of the scene, as seen in Figure 14-4. It's hard to think of any better way than mounting a GoPro on a headband or harness and walking through a castle, stepping in a battlefield, or maneuvering through a cave.

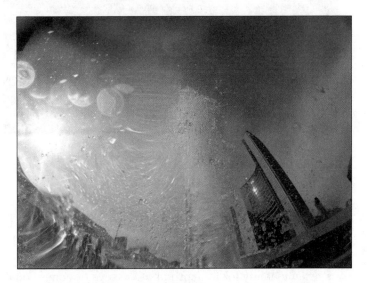

Figure 14-4: POV footage from the inside of a walk-through fountain.

# Professional Photography

The GoPro has found its way into many professional photographers' camera bags. It's fun to use when you're already comfortable with holding a camera, and that near-fish-eye view (I won't bicker over 10 degrees) lets you do some pretty creative stuff with still images and video.

If you're not already using a GoPro in your photography business, here are a few ways you can take advantage of it:

✓ **Take ultra-wide-angle pictures.** The GoPro allows you get really close to your subject to create a pleasantly distorted sense of perspective (see Figure 14-5).

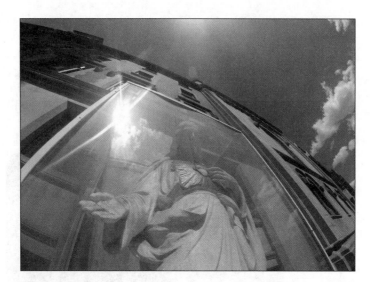

Figure 14-5: Wide-angle view of a statue of Jesus outside a New York City church.

✓ **Capture time-lapse footage.** Shoot a bunch of still images and play them as a movie, using the time-lapse setting on your GoPro and putting everything together in GoPro Studio Edit (see Chapter 11).

✓ **Capture video of yourself taking photographs.** This technique comes in especially handy for in-depth photo essays or commercial shoots.

✓ **Mount the camera remotely.** Sometimes it's easier to take the time to mount the camera on a pole or overhead railing than to climb and wait for the shot. After you mount it, you can watch what it's seeing using your smartphone or device.

✓ **Put the GoPro in harm's way.** Some situations make great photographs, but it's too dangerous to capture them directly. Maybe you're covering the running of the bulls at Pamplona or wanting to capture traffic on an interstate highway. Mounting the camera, getting away to a safe distance, and controlling the camera remotely prevents you from getting run over.

# Index

● *N* ●

# Notes

# Notes

# Notes

# Notes

# Notes

# Notes

# Notes

# About the Author

**John Carucci** has written about technology for more than 20 years and has published several books on the subject, including *Webinars For Dummies* and *Digital SLR Video and Filmmaking For Dummies.*

John has written more than 100 articles on photography, video, and technology. His work has appeared in many publications, including *American Photo, Popular Photography, PDN, Shutterbug, Photo Pro, PC Photo,* and others. He was also a contributing editor to *Popular Photography Magazine* from 2000 to 2002, writing about digital image and video technology. In addition, he was a contributing writer to *Photo Insider,* for which he wrote a bimonthly called "Digital Bytes" from 1998 to 2002.

Currently, John works as an entertainment news producer for Associated Press Television, where he covers music and theater. Those responsibilities include arranging and conducting studio interviews, covering field assignments (red carpets, news events, interviews, and so on), script writing, and editing both television packages and online segments. In addition to his television work, John also writes general news stories on the entertainment beat. Prior to that appointment, he was a photo editor covering sports, national, international, and features.

# Dedication

To my usual suspects, who make their way on stages, sets, and boats.

# Acknowledgements

Although it's always fun, it's not always easy to use a GoPro camera effectively. It's even more complicated when you try and explain how to do it. It takes a lot of support to get it done, so I need to thank some folks.

Let's start the folks at Wiley Publishing, starting with executive editor Steve Hayes for continuing to provide challenges, and for having the patience to continually modify the plan to accommodate my busy schedule. Thanks to editor Sarah Hellert for piecing this ever-evolving set of words and pictures together in a cohesive form.

I would also like to extend a great deal of gratitude to the folks at GoPro. There's nothing like getting sound advice from the people who make the camera. Special thanks to Kevin O'Leary and Jim Geduldick.

Thanks to my agent Carol Jelen for continuing to find great projects for me. Appreciate all your help.

And once again, thanks to Jillian, Anthony, and Alice for the necessary grounding.

## Publisher's Acknowledgments

**Executive Editor:** Steve Hayes

**Sr. Project Editor:** Sarah Hellert

**Copy Editor:** Kathy Simpson

**Technical Editor:** Robert Correll

**Editorial Assistant:** Paige Newman

**Sr. Editorial Assistant:** Cherie Case

**Project Coordinator:** Melissa Cossell

**Front Cover Image:** ©iStockphoto.com/ Paolo Cipriani

## Apple & Mac

iPad For Dummies,
6th Edition
978-1-118-72306-7

iPhone For Dummies,
7th Edition
978-1-118-69083-3

Macs All-in-One
For Dummies, 4th Edition
978-1-118-82210-4

OS X Mavericks
For Dummies
978-1-118-69188-5

## Blogging & Social Media

Facebook For Dummies,
5th Edition
978-1-118-63312-0

Social Media Engagement
For Dummies
978-1-118-53019-1

WordPress For Dummies,
6th Edition
978-1-118-79161-5

## Business

Stock Investing
For Dummies, 4th Edition
978-1-118-37678-2

Investing For Dummies,
6th Edition
978-0-470-90545-6

## Careers

Job Interviews
For Dummies, 4th Edition
978-1-118-11290-8

Job Searching with Social
Media For Dummies,
2nd Edition
978-1-118-67856-5

Personal Branding
For Dummies
978-1-118-11792-7

Resumes For Dummies,
6th Edition
978-0-470-87361-8

Starting an Etsy Business
For Dummies, 2nd Edition
978-1-118-59024-9

## Diet & Nutrition

Belly Fat Diet For Dummies
978-1-118-34585-6

Personal Finance
For Dummies, 7th Edition
978-1-118-11785-9

QuickBooks 2014
For Dummies
978-1-118-72005-9

Small Business Marketing
Kit For Dummies,
3rd Edition
978-1-118-31183-7

Mediterranean Diet
For Dummies
978-1-118-71525-3

Nutrition For Dummies,
5th Edition
978-0-470-93231-5

## Digital Photography

Digital SLR Photography
All-in-One For Dummies,
2nd Edition
978-1-118-59082-9

Digital SLR Video &
Filmmaking For Dummies
978-1-118-36598-4

Photoshop Elements 12
For Dummies
978-1-118-72714-0

## Gardening

Herb Gardening
For Dummies, 2nd Edition
978-0-470-61778-6

Gardening with Free-Range
Chickens For Dummies
978-1-118-54754-0

## Health

Boosting Your Immunity
For Dummies
978-1-118-40200-9

Diabetes For Dummies,
4th Edition
978-1-118-29447-5

Living Paleo For Dummies
978-1-118-29405-5

## Big Data

Big Data For Dummies
978-1-118-50422-2

Data Visualization
For Dummies
978-1-118-50289-1

Hadoop For Dummies
978-1-118-60755-8

## Language &
## Foreign Language

500 Spanish Verbs
For Dummies
978-1-118-02382-2

English Grammar
For Dummies, 2nd Edition
978-0-470-54664-2

French All-in-One
For Dummies
978-1-118-22815-9

German Essentials
For Dummies
978-1-118-18422-6

Italian For Dummies,
2nd Edition
978-1-118-00465-4

**Available in print and e-book formats.**

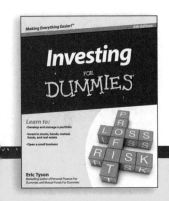

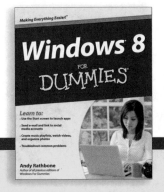

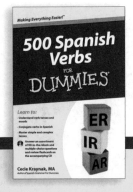

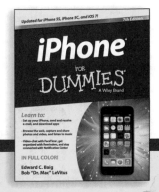

Available wherever books are sold. **For more information or to order direct visit www.dummies.com**

## Math & Science

Algebra I For Dummies,
2nd Edition
978-0-470-55964-2

Anatomy and Physiology
For Dummies, 2nd Edition
978-0-470-92326-9

Astronomy For Dummies,
3rd Edition
978-1-118-37697-3

Biology For Dummies,
2nd Edition
978-0-470-59875-7

Chemistry For Dummies,
2nd Edition
978-1-118-00730-3

1001 Algebra II Practice
Problems For Dummies
978-1-118-44662-1

## Microsoft Office

Excel 2013 For Dummies
978-1-118-51012-4

Office 2013 All-in-One
For Dummies
978-1-118-51636-2

PowerPoint 2013
For Dummies
978-1-118-50253-2

Word 2013 For Dummies
978-1-118-49123-2

## Music

Blues Harmonica
For Dummies
978-1-118-25269-7

Guitar For Dummies,
3rd Edition
978-1-118-11554-1

iPod & iTunes
For Dummies, 10th Edition
978-1-118-50864-0

## Programming

Beginning Programming
with C For Dummies
978-1-118-73763-7

Excel VBA Programming
For Dummies, 3rd Edition
978-1-118-49037-2

Java For Dummies,
6th Edition
978-1-118-40780-6

## Religion & Inspiration

The Bible For Dummies
978-0-7645-5296-0

Buddhism For Dummies,
2nd Edition
978-1-118-02379-2

Catholicism For Dummies,
2nd Edition
978-1-118-07778-8

## Self-Help & Relationships

Beating Sugar Addiction
For Dummies
978-1-118-54645-1

Meditation For Dummies,
3rd Edition
978-1-118-29144-3

## Seniors

Laptops For Seniors
For Dummies, 3rd Edition
978-1-118-71105-7

Computers For Seniors
For Dummies, 3rd Edition
978-1-118-11553-4

iPad For Seniors
For Dummies, 6th Edition
978-1-118-72826-0

Social Security
For Dummies
978-1-118-20573-0

## Smartphones & Tablets

Android Phones
For Dummies, 2nd Edition
978-1-118-72030-1

Nexus Tablets
For Dummies
978-1-118-77243-0

Samsung Galaxy S 4
For Dummies
978-1-118-64222-1

## Samsung Galaxy Tabs
For Dummies
978-1-118-77294-2

## Test Prep

ACT For Dummies,
5th Edition
978-1-118-01259-8

ASVAB For Dummies,
3rd Edition
978-0-470-63760-9

GRE For Dummies,
7th Edition
978-0-470-88921-3

Officer Candidate Tests
For Dummies
978-0-470-59876-4

Physician's Assistant Exam
For Dummies
978-1-118-11556-5

Series 7 Exam For Dummies
978-0-470-09932-2

## Windows 8

Windows 8.1 All-in-One
For Dummies
978-1-118-82087-2

Windows 8.1 For Dummies
978-1-118-82121-3

Windows 8.1 For Dummies
Book + DVD Bundle
978-1-118-82107-7

**e** **Available in print and e-book formats.**

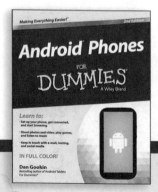

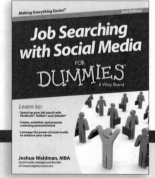

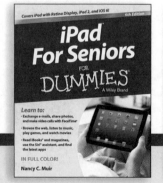

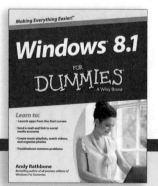

Available wherever books are sold. **For more information or to order direct visit www.dummies.com**

# Take Dummies with you everywhere you go!

Whether you are excited about e-books, want more from the web, must have your mobile apps, or are swept up in social media, Dummies makes everything easier.

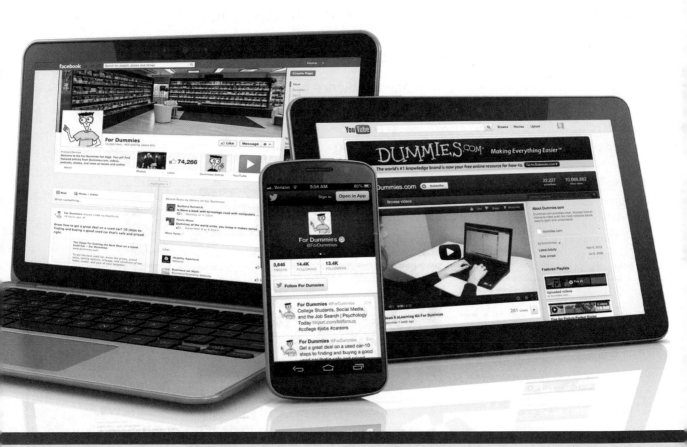

For Dummies is the global leader in the reference category and one of the most trusted and highly regarded brands in the world. No longer just focused on books, customers now have access to the For Dummies content they need in the format they want. Let us help you develop a solution that will fit your brand and help you connect with your customers.

## Advertising & Sponsorships

Connect with an engaged audience on a powerful multimedia site, and position your message alongside expert how-to content.

Targeted ads • Video • Email marketing • Microsites • Sweepstakes sponsorship

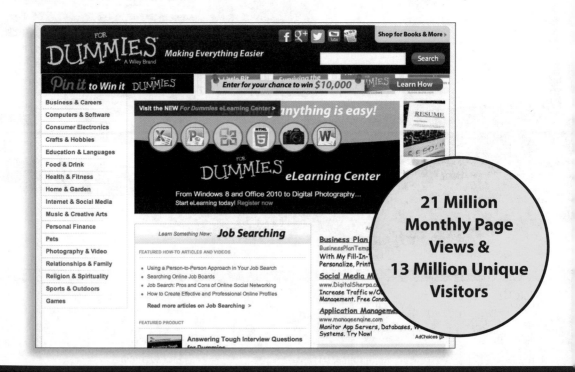

21 Million Monthly Page Views & 13 Million Unique Visitors

# Custom Publishing

Reach a global audience in any language by creating a solution that will differentiate you from competitors, amplify your message, and encourage customers to make a buying decision.

## Apps • Books • eBooks • Video • Audio • Webinars

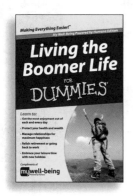 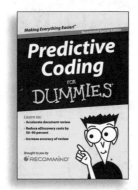 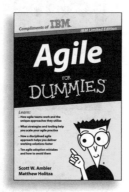 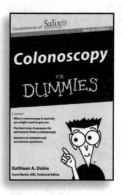

# Brand Licensing & Content

Leverage the strength of the world's most popular reference brand to reach new audiences and channels of distribution.

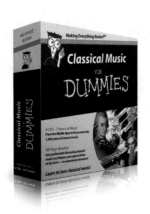 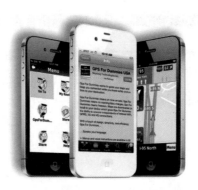 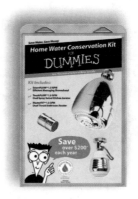 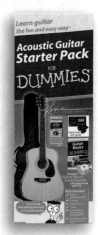

## For more information, visit www.Dummies.com/biz

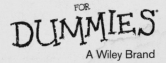

# Dummies products make life easier!

- DIY
- Consumer Electronics
- Crafts

- Software
- Cookware
- Hobbies

- Videos
- Music
- Games
- and More!

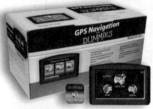

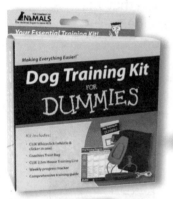

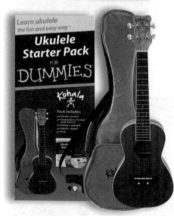

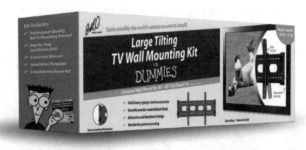

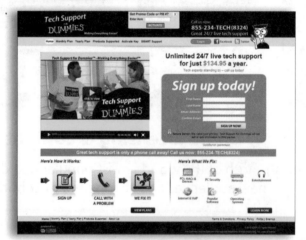

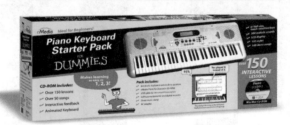

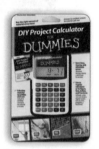

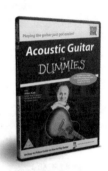

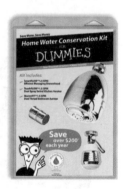

For more information, go to **Dummies.com** and search the store by category.

FOR **DUMMIES**®

A Wiley Brand